SCALE WITH **SPEED**

# SCALE WITH
# SPEED

The #1 Formula For
Massive Success in
Today's Marketplace

## JUDGE GRAHAM

NEW YORK

LONDON • NASHVILLE • MELBOURNE • VANCOUVER

# SCALE WITH **SPEED**
## The #1 Formula For Massive Success in Today's Marketplace

Published in New York, New York, by Morgan James Publishing. Morgan James is a trademark of Morgan James, LLC. www.MorganJamesPublishing.com

The Morgan James Speakers Group can bring authors to your live event. For more information or to book an event visit The Morgan James Speakers Group at www.TheMorganJamesSpeakersGroup.com.

ISBN 978-1-64279-140-2  paperback
ISBN 978-1-64279-141-9  eBook
Library of Congress Control Number: 2018907126

In an effort to support local communities, raise awareness and funds, Morgan James Publishing donates a percentage of all book sales for the life of each book to Habitat for Humanity Peninsula and Greater Williamsburg.

Get involved today! Visit
www.MorganJamesBuilds.com

# Dedication

To my wife Jordan Graham, who has stood by my side through the good, the bad, and the ugly. When I was at my lowest of lows, she was my rock and the cheerleader who kept pushing me forward. We are a team and without her encouragement, love, and support I would not be where I am today.

To my business partner Ernie "Rocco" Capobianco, along with John Holmes, Gabe Winslow, Jim Badum, Marian Leonard, Mim Davis and all the hundreds of teammates who have been part of the growth and exits of our companies, I am so thankful for each one of you. I truly understand that without an amazing team, you cannot achieve your dreams.

To my parents Nola and Rod Graham, without your steadfast belief and support that I could accomplish anything, I would never have had my "Make It Happen" drive and work ethic.

To Ruby Morning, my godmother, your love and belief that I was the best at everything I was doing or would do gave me my confidence to become the person I am today. I miss you every day and know you are always with me

To my mother-in-law Janet McKnight and extended family, thank you all for always supporting and understanding all the countless events and birthdays I missed in order to chase my dreams.

And to my amazing sons Jake and Jett, you are my inspiration to always charge forward.

# Table of Contents

# Foreword

## By Sharon L. Lechter

Speed is the new currency.

Today, everyone expects things to happen instantly. Thanks to technology, that's becoming increasingly possible. Expectations are constantly being raised.

No longer is it acceptable to respond to messages in 24 hours—instant responses are expected within minutes of receiving a message. Wait a week for an order to arrive? Amazon Prime members know they can get it that very afternoon or within two days at the most; that's the new delivery standard. Wait for the morning newspaper to arrive to get the latest news? No need. You can track events that occur worldwide online within a moment or two of it occurring.

What worked before is no longer effective, including how to scale a profitable business. Speed to market is essential to build a business and sustain its success.

There are a lot of so-called gurus and coaches now offering to teach you how to build a scalable business. Some promise that learning to deliver potent speeches is the key to success. Others want to teach you how to change your mindset, how to attract abundance, or how to use Facebook ads to drive traffic to your website.

All of those are good skills to have. But on their own, they aren't enough to achieve the big results you deserve—to be wildly successful, not just marginally successful. That won't happen if all you're doing is raising your visibility a little or investing some of your marketing dollars in promotion.

Surprisingly, to play big you really need to get clear about your strengths. Focus on what you or your business does best and then leverage that. Find a niche and then go all in.

That may sound scary to some of you. Giving up opportunities can bring up fear—fear of making the wrong decision, of missing out on other opportunities, and of failure. Taking a chance to achieve massive success takes courage, that's for sure.

I certainly felt that kind of fear when I decided to leave the Rich Dad Company after co-authoring *Rich Dad Poor Dad* and 14 other Rich Dad books and 10 years of building the business into the largest personal finance brand in the world. I thought Rich Dad would be my legacy but when I no longer agreed with the direction the business was taking, I made the difficult decision to leave.

The funny thing is, when you leave opportunities behind that you've outgrown, new ones often appear to fill the void. That's exactly what happened for me. Just a few months after parting ways with Rich Dad, I received a call asking me to be on then-President George Bush's first President's Advisory Council on Financial Literacy. Then, shortly after that, I was asked to partner with the Napoleon Hill Foundation on a book, *Three Feet From Gold*, which has led to a series of collaborations.

I took a chance to break away from what had become a limiting business relationship and discovered there were so many other opportunities out there for me. Sometimes you have to close one door for other doors of opportunity to open for you.

That's what you need to do, too. Do you feel that life has more in store for you? Do you feel energized by what you are doing? Are you ready to build your own business that aligns with your personal mission?

If you want to grow a scalable business, there has never been a better time to do it. It doesn't even need to be a massive empire—it can be a lean, high profit venture. And to do that, you need to get clear about your goals and how your business can help you reach them. Then you need to go all in, as quickly as possible.

It's kind of ironic that in order to move quickly, you also need to create systems and processes that will reduce wasted time and energy and enable fast progress. But those business systems and processes create the very fuel that allows your business to scale and soar.

Fortunately, *Scale With Speed* will help you do just that. You'll learn how to get clear about your personal and business goals, how to use those goals to develop a strategy for growth, to weed out initiatives that aren't serving your best and highest purpose, and then make progress at warp speed, to overtake and pass any competition.

In reading this book allow yourself to chart your own course to success.

**Sharon L. Lechter**, Author of *Think and Grow Rich for Women*, co-author of *New York Times* bestseller *Rich Dad Poor Dad*, 14 other books in the Rich Dad series, *Three Feet From Gold* and *Outwitting the Devil*.

# Introduction

I bet you've read plenty of business books—books that emphasize the importance of methodical planning and strategy and promotion and hiring and finance. Titles that promise that if you do x, y, and z just right, you'll succeed.

This isn't one of those books.

Yes, there's certainly value in carefully planning your business's growth trajectory, but I've found a better way—a way that won't let you get bogged down in planning out every step of your entrepreneurial journey. Because the truth is, it's not going to go how you think it will. It never does.

I'm going to teach you a proprietary formula and process to scale your business fast. It's a process that will enable you to make efficient decisions quickly, which will change the course of your business growth. It's one that's made me millions and can make millions for you, too.

I've found it makes more sense to focus on speed than thinking through the minutiae of how you want your business to be run. If you can work faster, you can achieve so much more than the entrepreneur who has spent months working on his business plan, calculating the most effective marketing budget, hiring rock star employees, investing in SEO, and attracting outside money. They may have the best-laid plans, but if they're working at the typical corporate pace, they'll be out of business soon.

You, on the other hand, will be light years ahead. By focusing on results alone, and following the principles in this book, you can achieve so much more than the teams of MBAs hunched over their spreadsheets.

## The Value of SPEED

I call it the SPEED formula: Start with your end game, Pick your niche, Execute with speed, Energize your culture, and Dominate your top priorities.

It's not complicated. Unlike other business books, I'm not going to overwhelm you with equations and multi-step processes or try and convince you that your mindset is all that matters. What matters is getting clear about what you're working toward, zeroing in on what you or your company is good at, making progress as fast as humanly possible, getting everyone on your team excited about the possibilities success will bring, and then staying focused on your goal.

You may think you're already working quickly. You're not. Sure, you may be progressing faster than some of your competitors but that doesn't mean you're working as fast as you could, or that you're working fast enough to be the market leader. That's where I want you to be. It's where I know you can be.

Why should you do it my way?

Because any other way is going to leave you disappointed with the results you get. The market is moving so fast that many companies are falling behind, only they don't know it yet. Today, if you're not first, you're last. Fortunately, I've proven that focusing on speed can get you where you want to go. My way is the path to scalable business growth faster than you thought possible. It's the path to profitability and financial independence.

Now, I'm not an academician or a researcher, I'm a practitioner. I'm a serial entrepreneur. I've been where you are right now, whether it's starting up and not sure of where you're headed, or maybe already in business and trying to figure out what's going to turn things around, or riding high and wanting to continue to build on your success so you have a valuable asset you can sell.

Yes, I have a successful track record of growing companies and selling them for multi- and hundreds-of-millions of dollars. I've also worked 100-hour weeks, struggling to turn around a failing business and then having to file for personal bankruptcy because I hadn't yet figured out what really mattered—speed.

You'll be ahead of where I was once you listen to what I have to share.

## Why You Need to Read this Book

I've written this book to share the mistakes I've made in my career thus far, the failures I survived, and the ultimate successes I've had, so you know you're not alone. If I can do it, you can do it.

This book isn't philosophical or theoretical, it's not a parable describing a fictional scenario, and it's not an anthology of interviews with people telling you sometimes conflicting advice. This is my story. It can also be your story, with a very happy ending if you implement the way I teach you to.

It's meant to be a fast-paced read so that you can quickly get to what's important—taking action. At the end of each chapter, in the section named "Speed Read," you'll find short summaries of the most important points.

My goal in sharing what I've learned is to create a movement of positivity, productivity, and profitability. It's to save you from many of the errors I made and give you a leg up as you scale.

Let's get going!

# Part 1

# Start with Your End Game

*"You don't have a business if you don't have an end game."*
— **Judge Graham**

You are not running a real business until you know your end game. That is, what do you hope to do with your business in the future? How will you get the most value from it?

If you were to retire today, is your business at a point where it can operate without you and still provide enough positive cash flow to maintain the lifestyle you want for the rest of your life? Would other companies be interested in acquiring your business for millions of dollars if you put it up for sale today?

If you answered "no" to both of these questions, don't be discouraged. Once you learn the SPEED formula, you'll be in a position to answer "yes."

So, let's dive-in on the "S" part of the SPEED formula: Start with your end game.

# What it Means to Scale with Speed

Speed is the new currency – it determines your success. We're living in a technology-driven, global economy that is 24/7/365. That's a fact. And if you can't be responsive and keep up with the pace of technology and innovation, your business will fail. Operating with speed is the framework that will drive successful growth.

Companies that learn to leverage speed gain an insurmountable competitive advantage. Those that can't, go bankrupt.

If you're not able to keep up, making decisions and executing faster than your competition, you're out of business. Period. Twenty-four percent of all startups fail in the first year and 48 percent fail by year two, says the SBA. Your odds of sticking around are about 50 percent, but your odds of tremendous success are far lower. You need to scale with speed to reap real financial rewards.

You're in a high-stakes battle for profits. Focusing on productivity improvements, efficiency gains, and hiring strategies simply isn't enough. You need to create processes that compress time and enable you to leapfrog other companies in your space.

This book is about scaling yourself and your business in an ever-changing world. It's a scary world that's moving faster than ever. If you can't keep up, you'll fail.

## Have a Sense of Urgency

This was never clearer to me than right after I joined the company that had acquired my startup, back in 2015. We had gone from being a small fish in a big pond to a moderate-sized fish that now looked even tastier to larger predators. The market was in a feeding frenzy, with large agencies buying up smaller ones left and right.

We wanted to be bought. We also knew that the feeding frenzy would end in the not-too-distant future. We needed to prepare to be acquired or get left behind, squeezed out of the market, quite literally. We had to act fast.

From Day One, my focus at the company was on positioning us to be bought by a larger agency. I did that by analyzing the market we were in and identifying a pain point that no one else was addressing. Then I studied the top-performing agencies as my role models, mimicked their operating practices, and created an entirely new solution in the marketplace that went beyond what any existing agencies offered. We created a niche we could dominate.

I had a heightened sense of urgency because of my personal experience in my last company; I had been days away from selling it when we lost our largest client. The deal fell apart and took months to piece back together. I didn't want to lose another opportunity because we weren't ready to move when a buyer indicated interest.

Within a matter of months, the largest agency in our industry—we were number 2—had two bidders trying to buy it. We knew that meant that the losing bidder would likely turn its attention to us, the second-largest agency. As soon as the other deal was signed, we wanted to be ready to woo the unsuccessful bidder.

That's exactly what happened. They lost out, wanted to quickly move on to their Plan B, which was acquiring us, and because we were primed and ready to move, the negotiations and due diligence were done in record time.

Because we were ready, we were even more appealing as an acquisitions candidate to the buyer. And because we'd been prepping, we could promise the deal would take less than half the time to close. Speed was on our side.

Not only did our preparations and speed make the deal possible, but it raised our value. The purchase price of many hundreds of millions of dollars we accepted was higher than we had initially expected. Had we waited for overtures of interest, it's possible the buyer would have expanded their set of acquisition candidates, reducing our negotiating power.

More importantly, speed allowed us to stay relevant—to stay in business. That's becoming increasingly challenging.

### The Need for Speed

In the business world today, speed is the new big, according to the Boston Consulting Group. It's the straight path to market domination, aggressive growth, and profitability.

As a society, everything is moving so much faster today than it did 10 or 20 years ago. Bloomberg View columnist Barry Ritholtz eloquently made that clear in an article in 2017:

> "The *Wall Street Journal* noted it took the landline telephone 75 years to hit 50 million users. Vala Afshar, the 'chief digital

evangelist' for Salesforce.com Inc., tweeted that it took airplanes 68 years, the automobile 62 years, light bulbs 46 years, and television 22 years to hit the same user milestones. But to really see how the pace of change has accelerated, consider the impact of technology since 2000. YouTube, Facebook and Twitter hit that 50-million user mark in four, three and two years, respectively. That may sound astonishing when compared with cars, television and light bulbs, but it's nothing when compared with the Angry Birds app, which took a mere 35 days.

Technology has hastened the pace of change and made possible mind-blowing innovations and breakthroughs. It has also made delays and a slower pace of work a major disadvantage. Can't keep up? You're out of business.

## Changes Around Us

This is even truer for companies that are trying to scale—to grow exponentially. The slower you move, the harder it is to scale.

And competition is springing up all around you. According to the Global Entrepreneurship Monitor, three new startups are formed every second. Almost nine more were formed since you started reading this sentence.

It's almost overwhelming.

Just look at the flow of information on social media, for example. The pace of information-sharing continues to accelerate. According to Domo, every 60 seconds:

- Facebook users share nearly 2.5 million posts
- Twitter users tweet almost 300,000 times
- Instagrammers upload close to 220,000 photos

We're seeing similar increases in communication. According to an article in Lifewire, the average office worker receives 121 emails a day and sends out 40. That number is also increasing, according to the Radicati Group, which found that an average of 205 billion emails were sent daily in 2015. Just two years later, that average had climbed to 269 billion—an increase of 31 percent.

Exponential growth and progress is happening all around us.

Once you get ahead, it's time to scale. Speed and scale are your one-two punch.

Scaling with speed is a chance at massive success.

*The average office worker receives 121 emails a day and sends out 40.*

While two-thirds of startups won't last a decade, according to the SBA, a small fraction will hit the jackpot. According to the Kauffman Foundations' report "The Constant: Companies that Matter," of the 552,000 new businesses formed each year, only between 125 and 250 will ever hit $100 million in revenue. That's .02 to .045 percent that scale with speed.

I've actually experienced both success and failure in business. My first venture, which I started while still in college at Texas Christian University, was in web design. With the help of my business partner and best friend, we grew steadily and quickly to the point where we had 30 employees and thousands of square feet of space, but not enough recurring revenue. We couldn't scale, I learned too late. Our business model simply wouldn't allow it.

## Start Where You Are Now

Don't think that you have to run a massive company to benefit from the principles of scaling with speed. In fact, the smaller your business, the more you have to gain.

Of the 28 million small businesses in the U.S., reports the U.S. Census Bureau, more than 22 million are single-person operations—meaning they have no employees. These solo operators actually have the greatest opportunity to scale—to grow their businesses from ventures dependent solely on the owner to enterprises that can continue to grow without daily involvement from the owner.

There are four requirements for scaling with speed:

1. You serve a niche market
2. You have a quality product or service
3. You have an end game in mind
4. You have to be fully committed and take massive action

If you have those, you're ready to go.

## How to Scale

Scaling is the new business objective. Forget revenue targets and headcount, companies today want to achieve transformative growth. They don't want slow-and-steady, iterative growth. No, they want revolutionary up-leveling.

Leapfrogging ahead so quickly provides a massive competitive advantage and allows companies to take over a particular market or niche. Gradual growth is expected—your competition is counting on it—and offers no advantage to speak of.

Of course, scaling is more difficult than pure profit improvement or business expansion.

When your company is generating, say, $250,000 or $500,000 in revenue, being able to scale means hitting $1 million next year and $4 million the year after that. It's the opposite of incremental growth, where you increase revenue from $250,000 to $400,000 to $600,000 and beyond. That takes much more time and often slows the more you grow.

Successful scaling requires a framework that methodically propels the company forward.

Fortunately, I've done it. I know what it takes to catapult a company's revenues. One company that brought me in as a partner was making $600,000 annually at the time. In less than six years, we were at $30+ million using the Scale with Speed formula.

It makes scaling possible.

## Outsource the Non-Essentials

Multi-million dollar brand Birch Benders, a natural and organic manufacturer and marketer of vegan, paleo, gluten-free, and high protein pancakes started as a two-person operation testing batches in the duo's rental unit's kitchen. Today the purveyors of pancakes are nearing the eight figure mark in sales, because they were willing to do all of the things necessary to scale with speed.

First, they chose a niche market. Actually, a niche within a niche—a vegan, paleo, gluten-free, and high protein food product that appeals to a thin slice of the consumer segment consisting of people with food allergies and dietary restrictions. Then they chose a breakfast product within that niche—pancakes.

The nature of their product almost requires that it be of the best quality, eliminating ingredients that cause issues for those who eat it and replacing them with harder-to-find alternatives.

Their end game was to roll out a national brand and co-founders Lizzi Ackerman and her husband Matt LaCasse were clear about that.

They took massive action and stuck with it until the company was successful. They worked with Whole Foods to figure out how to best package the mixes, which only require water, to make the price point appealing to the largest number of buyers, they explained in the book *The Million-Dollar, One-Person Business*. After several rounds of testing they settled on 16-ounce packages that retail for about $5.99.

They also turned manufacturing over to a copacker, rather than continuing to try and make the products themselves, to take advantage of economies of scale the larger organization could provide them. Finding one initially that was willing to produce "tiny" runs of 1,000 packages "was challenging," says Ackerman. But copacking savings coupled with savings from being able to buy raw materials in bulk have helped Birch Benders steadily scale.

They started with an idea for a product, found a niche, tested it relentlessly, and then executed, steadily building their company without investing unnecessarily in labor and leased space, making it easier to reach profitability faster.

## The Quickening Pace of Life

While having a framework to follow is part of the equation here, speed is a critical component. Today you can't aim to simply adapt to market moves, you need to be the market mover if you want to be successful. The marketplace doesn't reward followers nearly as much as the leaders.

Audiences have come to expect the latest-and-greatest innovation is right around the corner. Apple's iPhone is the poster child for setting expectations that a newer, more fabulous model will be released each fall. They continually raise the bar, making it harder for the competition to catch up. Apple is so far out front in terms of innovation and new product development that it's nearly impossible for someone to unseat them. But the reality is that if their pace of innovation slows, their fickle customers will consider looking elsewhere for a new cell phone.

Fortunately, it's unlikely that will happen. Apple has created an internal corporate culture centered on speed and innovation. Its own performance standards are higher than those of consumers, making it possible for Apple to stay ahead of customer expectations. Its employees are focused on delivering the newest, coolest technology on a regular basis.

At the same time, corporate lifespans are shrinking: "The 33-year average tenure of companies on the S&P 500 in 1964 narrowed to 24 years by 2016 and is forecast to shrink to just 12 years by 2027," according to Innosight's biennial corporate longevity forecast.

## A Case-in-Point

To find an example of a company that is scaling with speed you need only look at Slack, the enterprise collaboration tool that in four years has gained 6.8 million daily active users worldwide, nearly one-third of which are paid users. It is already valued at $5.1 billion and a March 2018 write-up in *Computerworld* asserted that Slack "could replace email in the future."

Since its inception, Slack has been operating at warp speed. By the end of its first year, Slack was deemed "the fastest growing startup ever," by the Global Big Data Conference.

It then became the fastest company to reach a $2 billion valuation, which the CEO, Stewart Butterfield, credited in part to the market we're in: "Over the last five to seven years, companies have been able to scale really quickly in terms of revenue…the scale of revenue growth is unprecedented." It took Slack 1.25 years to hit $1 billion in revenue and 1.71 years to hit $2 billion—the fastest sprint on record, according to Business Insider.

Because of its pace of growth, Slack is considered a modern technology marvel. While its CEO acknowledges that someone else could come along and build a better Slack, he thinks it's unlikely due to the amount of customer feedback the company has gathered since its inception. Its ability to scale with speed has Slack on a trajectory that no company has been able to match thus far.

That's a tremendous competitive advantage.

## Speed Read

- Speed allows you to scale. Scale is all about exponential growth – how to do things fast that have exponential impact. Scale is all about growth. Any initiative you're implementing, you need to think about scale. You need to be thinking at a 10X level. Focus your time and effort on things that will have massive impact, to harness speed. If you're thinking too small, focusing on minor details, you're never going to scale.

- There are four requirements for scaling with speed: 1) You serve a niche market 2) You have a quality product or service 3) You have an end game in mind 4) You have to be fully committed and take massive action.

- To scale quickly you need to choose a niche, make a quality product or service, decide on an end game, and take sustained massive action immediately.

# Figure Out Your End Game

All successful businesses start with the end in mind. If you don't have an end game – a plan for how you're going to get out of your business - you don't have a real company, you have a job you've created for yourself.

Whether you've been in business for decades or are just starting up, you need to stop and think about where you're headed. How will you get back all the value you've invested in your company when you decide to exit?

There are really only four options for your end game. You can:

- Continue to keep and run it and pass it down to a family member or employee
- Position it to sell

- Merge it with another business
- Shut it down

Do you want to invest years of your time and effort to simply make a living or just get by? Are you tired of feeling like you give and give so much to your business and never feel like it gives back to you what you put in? I was there in my first business and vividly remember what it was like.

I know what it feels like to get up every morning and put on a suit to go out knocking on doors in 100-degree heat. I know how tiring and uncomfortable that is. I sold website design services to businesses in my area and while I was great at it, I never felt like I could get ahead. I'd sell dozens of websites each month but as soon as one project was done, we needed to replace it with a new client.

I was on a hamster wheel I couldn't get off of. I wasn't building a business, I had created a job for myself. If I stopped knocking on doors, our business would fold. It wasn't sustainable. In truth, it wasn't a business at all.

Your business needs to be an asset you can sell or draw massive income from every month.

Your business end game is a lot like a travel destination. When heading out on vacation, you typically decide where you want to go and what route you're going to take to get there before you leave home. Are you going to the Cape for the weekend? To Rodeo Drive for some shopping? Or maybe Miami for some sun? Where do you want to be at the end of your travels?

Your business end game requires the same kind of thinking. Where do you want to end up and what steps are you going to take to get maximum value from your business journey? Are you hoping to build a conglomerate you can sell off to the highest bidder? Do you want to create a concept you can franchise and live off royalties? Are you investing in a business you hope will stay in the family for generations?

There's no wrong answer here, only what's right *for you*.

The SPEED formula is designed to allow you to achieve your end game, so let's dive-in and get started!

> *Your business needs to be an asset you can sell or draw massive income from every month.*

## What's Your Vision for Your Business?

First you need to decide what you want out of your business – what you want your life to look like. A business is a vehicle for giving you that dream lifestyle. And a vision board is a tool that allows you to brainstorm how you want to live.

A vision board is an exercise that forces your brain to imagine your ideal life, so that you can work backwards from that vision to figure out what you need to do to achieve it. And once you see how hard you have to work to earn that $4 million home or that yacht, you may want to recalibrate. It's a gut check. If your vision and your business goals aren't in sync, you need to really think about how badly you want that life. Your vision board needs to resonate with you for it to work.

I usually start by creating an end game vision board. This is a one-page sheet of paper that I create for my business that outlines the following:

- Why did you start this business, or why do you continue to run it?
- What do you want the business to give back to you in:
  - One year
  - Two years

o   Three years
o   Five years
- What will it feel like to achieve these goals?

The answers to these questions sets performance targets for my company.

## Create Your Own Vision Board

To help you see what a vision board could look like, here's an example of one approach for the owner of a new home security company. It's just an example to help you think about what should be on your vision board.

- Why did you start this business?
  - o   I want to provide peace of mind to my customers, to allow them to sleep easier at night, knowing that my video security software, cameras, and monitoring services are protecting their homes.
  - o   I want to create financial freedom for myself and a more comfortable lifestyle for my family, with less stress about money.
- What do you want the business to give back to you?
  - o   Year 1—A salary of $100k
  - o   Year 2—A new Tesla and a $200k-per-year salary
  - o   Year 3—A new $700k home, three $10k vacations, and $300k in salary
  - o   Year 5—Sell the business and personally put $5 million+ in my bank account
- Imagine you've achieved your stated goals
  - o   What does it feel like to have accomplished your goals?
  - o   How is that future feeling different from what you feel today?

o What are some words that describe how you're feeling now that you've accomplished these goals?

## My Vision Board

My own vision board changes every year as I update it after achieving my personal goals. Early on my main goal was to establish a digital marketing agency to serve the Fortune 500. On my vision board I included the logos of several Fortune 500 companies I wanted to work with.

I also wanted to address why I was starting the business, which was to create financial freedom for myself and my family. So I included photos of money, a huge home, a Range Rover, skiing and beach vacations, gifts for my family members, and a Wall Street bull with a positive green arrow going up.

Granted, my motivations are primarily financial, and yours may not be. Maybe you want the flexibility to spend more time with your young children, or you want to be able to travel regularly—whatever your goals, think about what images you associate with those, and then glue them onto your vision board.

## Feeling Successful

Believe it or not, visualizing what it will feel like to achieve your goals is an important step in making that goal attainable. Along with envisioning what that success will look like, what it will feel like is equally important.

So when you fast forward and picture what obtaining your goals feels like, pay attention to what your body is telling you. Are you feeling:

- Energized
- Excited
- A sense of purpose
- Relief

- Fulfilled
- Satisfied
- Proud

Ideally, you're feeling something akin to nirvana.

### Be Specific, Be Clear

Research has shown that the more specific you are about each goal, the greater your odds of achieving it. So rather than saying, for example, that your goal is to earn "Enough money to pay my bills," calculate exactly what that number is. Put that figure on your vision board.

If you want a Tesla, get specific about which model and color you want sitting in your driveway.

If you want a new home, find a picture of your ideal place.

*Find images that reflect what you're working toward.*

Then, put all of those pictures and supporting words onto a piece of foam core or poster board. Combine words that represent your goals and images of them on that board and hang it somewhere prominent, where you'll see it every day. That might be directly across from your desk. Or it could be in your bedroom, so it's the last thing you see as you drift off to sleep and the first thing that catches your attention in the morning.

You want this as your daily reminder and motivator of why you started the business and what you are working towards. Never lose sight of your dreams and goals or they will never come true.

## Developing SPEED Habits

Looking at your vision board daily is critical, which is why I want you to place it where you'll see it repeatedly throughout the day.

Start your day by looking at your vision board and thinking about what you're working toward and how it will feel to achieve everything you're working toward.

At the end of the day, before bed, look again at your vision board and reflect on what you did that day that got you closer to your goals. How does that progress feel?

If you can, put your vision board somewhere out in the open, where you'll see it frequently throughout the day. You could make copies of it and put one in a frame on your desk and have another one in your bedroom mirror. Or you could carry it with you in your wallet and pull it out before each meeting.

Another option is to digitize your vision board, or create one using online tools, and look at it on your smartphone or computer throughout the day. A couple of websites where you can create vision boards online include DreamItAlive and Corkulous, which looks and functions like an online cork board. By creating digital vision boards, you can tap into them from wherever you are.

Promise me you'll take time every day to think about what it will mean to you to achieve those goals. How fulfilled will you feel? How satisfied will you be? Look at your vision board, visualize achieving all of the goals you have on it, and then say an incantation—an affirmation spoken out loud. Sometimes speaking your goals is what flips a switch from being skeptical to being a believer. It's important.

It may sound crazy, but Tony Robbins uses incantations to change his mindset and focus on where he's headed. He transformed his life—literally—by talking himself into believing that he was meant for better things, that he was on his way to being wildly successful. And he was right.

## Speaking Your Success

Positive statements about yourself and what you're working toward that you repeat in your head can have a tremendous impact on your mindset and attitude. You can have all the goals in the world but unless you truly believe that you can accomplish them, you'll fail. Affirmations serve as psychological triggers that help your brain believe that you can be successful.

Examples of positive affirmations include:

- "I am building a successful company."
- "My business is headed for massive growth and success."
- "New business ideas come to me daily."
- "My business provides for all of my family's needs."
- "I attract ideal clients with ease."

When you verbalize an affirmation, saying it aloud, it becomes a powerful incantation. Says Tony Robbins:

"With incantations, not only are you speaking words of empowerment, you are using your body and your voice. You are changing your physiology and changing your state, and this can change everything."

## Don't Mock Vision Boards

I know some of you are rolling your eyes right now, wondering what in the world vision boards have to do with scaling a multi-million dollar business. Don't be a hater.

Vision boards make intangible goals tangible—visible. It's much easier to work toward a goal that you can picture and feel. That's why they're so valuable.

Did you hear the story about actor Jim Carrey and the check he wrote himself for $10 million? It was 1985 and he was barely making ends meet, at one point living out of his car, and he promised himself that at Thanksgiving in 10 years, he would be able to cash that $10 million check for "acting services rendered." He carried it with him in his wallet as a reminder of what he was working toward. And then shortly before Thanksgiving in 1995, he received word that he would earn $10 million to make the movie *Dumb and Dumber*.

Part of the secret behind vision boards is putting yourself in the right frame of mind to attract success. That means surrounding yourself with positive people who want to see you succeed. They help insulate and protect you from those who are jealous and who only want to see you fail, because it makes them feel better about their own situations.

All of these steps I've reviewed here are designed to help you start to determine your end game, visualize it, make clear why it's important, and then support it with incantations. It's a process that will help you scale with speed.

## Speed Read

- You need a vision board to crystallize your goals and make clear the effort you'll have to expend to reach them. Then you need to do a gut check to confirm that ideal life is what you're willing to work for. You may not want to work that hard. Better to know now.

- Your possible end game options include: 1) Selling your company to someone else 2) Handing it down to a family member or employee 3) Merging the company with another business 4) Shutting it down and walking away.
- Daily affirmations are a smart way to keep you motivated and focused on your goal.
- Your business needs to be an asset you can sell or draw massive income from every month.

# Match Your End Game
# with Your Business

Your vision board is your first step to matching your business and end game. That's a critical step to scaling with speed.

But your vision board is one of your early steps on the path to designing a profitable business that plays to your strengths. First, figure out how you want to live, then visualize it, express it with words and pictures on your vision board, and, finally, calculate what that lifestyle would cost. It's important to calculate this number; this is your reality check.

Think about how hard you want to work. Does that dollar figure scare you or motivate you? Are you all in, or do you want to scale back some of those plans? Because next, you're going to have to build a business to support that vision.

While it may seem frivolous to think about what you're going to do with the business you're building, it's not at all. Your long-term goals should drive how your business is structured, run, and handed off in the future. But how, exactly, you intend to hand off your company should influence the majority of the decisions you're making today.

You really have two major paths to choose from:

1. Build a lifestyle business that funds a comfortable personal life
2. Build an enterprise to sell off at a profit or hand down to your children or grandchildren

The end game you select—lifestyle or enterprise—will determine the path you should take and inform your decisions along the way.

If you realize you're going to have to work 100-hour weeks for years to accomplish your life goals and you decide that's not what you want, you need to choose a different end game. You need to reset your priorities on your vision board to align with what you want to do.

Now that you know what your end game is, it's time to decide if you are building a lifestyle business or a scalable business you can later sell or pass down to your kids. The SPEED formula can be applied to either, and once implemented will give you massive growth.

## Choose Your Path

Let me help you understand the difference between the two types of businesses, because it can get murky. Lifestyle businesses can remain high profit, smaller companies or they can scale and become enterprises. Enterprises are designed to scale quickly.

Did you ever watch or hear about the '70s TV show "Sanford & Son?" The star of the show was Fred Sanford who, together with his son and partner Lamont, ran a junk dealership. The two men would buy and resell cast-offs from local customers, generally for little or no profit. It was a struggling business, primarily because Fred Sanford was generally unwilling to work (it was a comedy).

Sanford & Son was a lifestyle business. It provided an income, limited as it was, for the two men to live, but there was too little revenue for it to become anything else.

Contrast that fictional business with real-life 1-800-GOT-JUNK. This national junk hauler started out as a one-person venture, when college student Brian Scudamore created a summer job for himself in Vancouver, Canada. He was struggling to find a way to earn an income in his home town back in 1989 and happened to spot an old trash removal truck going down the road. That sparked an idea and he decided to start his own trash removal service, which he named "The Rubbish Boys" and promised "We'll stash your trash in a flash."

Unlike Fred Sanford, however, Scudamore recognized the business's potential for growth. He changed the name to 1-800-GOT-JUNK in 1998 and began franchising the concept worldwide. The company now has more than 200 franchises in three countries.

## Reflect on Your Goals

When you started your business, you might have had certain aspirations. Maybe you wanted to hit $1 million in sales. Maybe you wanted to franchise the concept nationwide or be able to hire all your kids to work for you, making it a true family business. Or maybe you just wanted to make enough money to pay your bills and not have to worry as much about money.

There's no right or wrong answer here, only what's right for you given your personal situation. But there are some guidelines you can follow to determine which end game makes the most sense for you, or will yield the results you're hoping for.

Research conducted by Securian Financial Group discovered that 37 percent of business owners hope and plan to transfer their businesses to family members, including the next generation. Another 50 percent hope to sell their companies, either to internal stakeholders, such as employees or partners, or to external buyers. However, 72 percent have taken no steps to prepare for either step. That means it's unlikely they'll ever be able to follow through on either path, because they aren't looking ahead.

The fact that 72 percent of business owners have done nothing to plan for the future of their companies is both alarming and shocking to me. Have you heard the old adage that if you fail to plan you plan to fail? Well, this statistic proves that too few entrepreneurs are planning at all. To scale with speed, you have to first have a game plan.

 *Seventy-two percent of business owners have done nothing to plan for the future of their companies.*

### Compare Your Options

There are pros and cons for both types of business and your intended end game. Here are some advantages and disadvantages to help you decide what your long-term goal is:

### *Lifestyle business*

- You can grow a lifestyle business at your own pace, funding your lifestyle.
- You decide the level of effort you'll invest and how much time and money to invest in it.
- The success of the business is dependent to a large degree on your skills and abilities.
- Because it is based on your personal talents and ambitions, it takes longer to build this type of company into a multi-million-dollar venture—though it certainly is possible.
- To keep generating an income, you have to keep working.

- Limited by your involvement, lifestyle businesses are difficult to scale.

Many small businesses are lifestyle ventures, often providing a decent income to the owner. For example, a hairstylist who rents a chair in a beauty salon and serves his or her own clientele runs a lifestyle business—their income is 100% dependent on their ability to sell their products and services. A graphic designer who provides graphic design services to area businesses and whose capacity is limited by their own work speed runs a lifestyle business. Or a lawn service run by a business owner is also a lifestyle business if it serves a local area and is run by one or two owners.

A lifestyle business can be extremely satisfying and financially rewarding to the business owner. There's nothing wrong with owning a lifestyle business—unless your goal is to build a multi-million dollar empire that has value on its own. Then you want an enterprise.

However, the good news is that a lifestyle business can certainly become an enterprise, if that's what you decide you want for yourself.

### Enterprise

- An enterprise exists separate from the owner, providing fewer income limitations.
- By involving others in managing it, the owner loses some control, at least over day-to-day management.
- To scale, you need to invest more money in building an infrastructure that supports continued growth and expansion.
- You need more than 4-5 employees to scale.
- It's riskier for that reason; there's more at stake.
- More people need to be involved to fuel the growth.
- The potential payoff is much bigger.

Most larger companies are enterprises—businesses that were designed to continue to grow and scale independent of the owner. Companies like Walmart, UPS, McDonald's, Wells Fargo, or Apple, for example, are enterprises. Their ability to grow is not tied to any one individual worker—they can scale effortlessly.

By the same token, a hairstylist who, instead of renting a chair inside someone else's salon, buys or leases real estate to hold their own salon, which then rents chairs out to other stylists, is running an enterprise. The salon can grow beyond that one location and employ as many stylists as the market demands. By the same token, a single graphic designer can decide to build a remote team worldwide and pursue major contracts with organizations around the globe—evolving into an enterprise from a lifestyle business. And a local lawn care provider can decide to go big time—to scale with speed—and invest in a fleet of lawn care vehicles and machinery in order to serve an entire metro area or region.

Enterprises have almost unlimited growth potential. And lifestyle businesses can become enterprises, but only if you decide that's what you want. Not every entrepreneur wants to run a large business.

In the short-term, either type of business can generate hundreds of thousands or even millions of dollars. But when you look long-term, decades down the road, your decision now will make a difference.

Honestly, if you choose to run a lifestyle business you can make lots of money in the short-term. But your end game is limited – you won't have a business to sell or hand down in the long-term. A lifestyle business isn't worth your time if you want to scale. If you want to grow a monster business to set you up for financial freedom, a lifestyle business isn't the way to go.

Anyone who chooses a lifestyle business has no chance of scaling. Period.

You have to decide if being a high school football star is how you want to be known or if you're aiming to be an NFL Hall of Famer.

Business is no different. It will take an extraordinary amount of training, work, focus, and mental toughness to win at the highest level.

My goals early on were monetary. I wanted a Porsche, a Range Rover, Rolex watches, a huge home, and Air Jordans. When I was in grade school, I really wanted Air Jordans but they were too expensive. We couldn't afford them.

So when I sold my first company, I bought 14 pairs of Air Jordans — all styles and patterns. I tried to make up for all the pairs I didn't have when I was little.

Since then my mindset has shifted, however. It's not completely focused on acquiring stuff. But at first, that's where my head was. That mindset led me to focus on building a monster company I could sell to attain financial freedom, so that's what I did. And then I did it again.

## Seven Business Characteristics You Need to Scale and Sell

If you've decided that scaling with speed and building an enterprise is your desired end game, you'll want to be sure that your business has the following seven characteristics. These are the seven factors buyers will evaluate as they decide whether they're interested in owning your enterprise:

1. **Recurring or predictable revenue**. A buyer wants to see that you've been in business for a few years and that your revenue growth is steady and predictable, thanks to your recurring revenue.
2. **Diversified client base**. Buyers want to see that you're earning revenue from a large and diverse number of clients, rather than a handful—that's much more risky. No one account should represent more than 30 percent of your revenue.
3. **Big market with big opportunity**. Yes, you want to carve out a niche that you own, but that niche needs to represent

a sizeable market, or be able to be expanded and scaled into a larger opportunity.

4. **Earnings before interest, tax, depreciation and amortization (EBITDA) is 25+ percent**. Although EBITDA standards vary by industry, yours should be at least 15 percent.

5. **Year-over-year growth**. Buyers want to see that your venture is growing consistently.

6. **Solid management team**. Your company needs to be able to continue to grow and thrive when you are no longer associated with it. That means you need an experienced and talented management team in place to continue supporting the business under a new owner.

7. **Your business has scale**. Your business needs to be large enough to demonstrate that it can scale profitably. When considered together, the previous six characteristics should demonstrate that the company has considerable growth potential.

Now, don't get me wrong—both lifestyle and enterprise businesses are great. One isn't better than the other, unless your goal is to create a company with massive growth potential—then you want to build an enterprise. The principles I'm sharing with you here regarding scaling with SPEED are applicable to both an enterprise and lifestyle business.

### Speed Read

- You really have two major paths to choose from: 1) Build a lifestyle business that funds a comfortable personal life 2) Build an enterprise to sell off at a profit or hand down to your children or grandchildren.
- The 7 characteristics you need to scale and sell: 1) Recurring or predictable revenue 2) Diversified client base 3) Big market with big opportunity 4) Earnings before interest, tax, depreciation

and amortization (EBITDA) is 25+ percent 5) Year-over-year growth 6) Solid management team 7) Your business has scale.

- You can build a lifestyle business or an enterprise with the advice in this book, but if your goal is to create a monster business and gain financial freedom, then you need to build an enterprise business. A lifestyle business won't cut it.

# Part 2

# Pick Your Niche

*"Niche will get you rich."*
**– Judge Graham**

The most efficient and effective way to scale with speed is to select a market niche you can dominate. Trying to serve everyone with a huge selection of products and services only results in spreading your resources too thin; you'll end up selling to no one.

Instead, select a market niche—demographic, geographic, psychographic, product, or service—where you can position your company as the leader and win.

First you'll want to do some competitive intelligence gathering to determine what your strengths are relative to your competition and then to confirm that you can serve your chosen market better than any other business.

After you choose your niche, you'll want to strategize how best to create a recurring revenue stream that will allow your company to grow exponentially. Just offering a one-time-use product or service won't cut it when you're looking to scale quickly. You need to devise an approach that creates revenue automatically.

# Go an Inch Wide and a Mile Deep

Y ou'd think that, to build a successful business, generate more sales, and earn more money that you'd need to keep your business focus as general and broad as possible, right? You want to be the Walmart or Amazon of your industry, don't you?

Wrong. No, you don't.

We live in an age of specialists—a time when expertise is highly prized. Instead of hiring generalists who know a whole bunch about a lot of different topics, we'd much rather hire people or companies that specialize in the exact issue we face or product we want to buy. So instead of buying a desktop computer from a big box computer retailer, we'll order a machine configured specifically for high resolution video gaming. Or instead of taking our car to the auto mechanic down the street, we'll take it to a precision mechanic who specializes in our specific type of performance vehicle.

My first business, specializing in web design and development, wasn't niched, and that hurt us. We eventually went out of business because we lacked a differentiator. I ended up in debt and financially struggling. But that motivated me to do things different the next time around.

So I looked at my skillset and expertise, which was clearly digital marketing, and then looked to find the pain in the advertising marketplace. What did clients hate? What was frustrating them?

Then I saw it. Clients had two different agencies: an agency that bought digital media and an agency that created and managed their website. Clients spent a huge amount of time managing those two agencies, which were often pointing fingers at the other when asked why results weren't what had been expected. It was always the other guy's fault.

I decided to marry those two types of agencies into one. We handled both areas – digital media buys and building and optimizing websites. It will be faster and better, we promised potential clients. The market was eager to see if we could do what we promised. We did. We earned our first client a 300 percent increase in their results. From there we had no problem attracting more business, because we could clearly articulate our niche and prove our results.

Not every industry has clearly-defined niches. Medicine is one of a very few industries where niches are standard. If you have a cardiac issue, you see a cardiologist. If you get migraines, you see a neurologist. Everyone understands the importance of healthcare niches. Businesses are just now starting to see the light.

We prefer to work with experts. And while it may seem counterintuitive, carving out a well-defined niche will actually attract more customers faster, because it will be clear exactly when they need your products or services. Helping customers understand when they should turn to you is so much easier when your swim lane is extremely narrow.

There is a business in New York called Can Kings. It's a hole-in-the-wall shop that deals in recyclable cans. That's all. Instead of returning aluminum soda and beer cans and water bottles to a self-service machine at the supermarket, you can bring any amount of cans to Can Kings and they'll sort them for you and give you five cents a can. On some days of the week they'll even pay you a penny more than the automated machines will.

It's such a niche business that you might wonder if they could really survive, but the owners of Can Kings are actually thriving, with plans to open several new locations. Their niche is making them rich.

Or take Replacements, Ltd., which has been around for many years. Replacements buys and sells hard-to-find china, flatware, and crystal glassware. It's where you turn when you break that dinner plate from your antique china set that great Aunt Sally gave you years ago. Replacements is the middleman, buying china customers no longer want and reselling it to people who want to replace pieces in their sets that they've broken or lost.

It's a niche business for sure, and yet no one else dares compete with them. Those who used to are no longer in business. Sure, you can go to eBay and see if an individual seller has what you're after, but Replacements is the true specialist. They've gone an inch wide and a mile deep in their industry and you should too.

## The Benefit of Limited Focus

By specializing, you have the opportunity to perfect the process you use within your business. When you run a niche business, you have one main process to focus on. Let's say you run a car wash—you have one process within the car wash to monitor, maintain, and improve on. Or maybe you run an SAT (Standardized Aptitude Test) prep program—your sole focus is on training students to achieve a better score on the SAT.

By niching your business you can zero in on making sure your business process is the best it can be—that it delivers all that customers want and expect from you. Because you have a single process to pay attention to, you can easily introduce needed changes and improvements as needed.

Now consider if instead of running an SAT prep program you ran a tutoring company—you tutor students of all ages in all subjects. To do that, you have multiple subject matter experts on staff for elementary, middle, and high school students, covering nearly every age level. Your business is more of a generalist, not a specialist. You have more processes, more instructors, more teaching styles, and more potential personality conflicts and errors. In this case, diversity is not your friend.

You're also competing with national players like Sylvan and Kumon, who have already perfected their business process and are scaling. A better approach would be to choose a niche that's a subset of what Sylvan and Kumon offer, like foreign language tutoring or preparation for Advanced Placement (AP) tests at the end of the year.

By choosing a niche that is super narrow, but extremely deep, it's easier to establish your credibility and expertise than it is to try and be all things to all people.

## Dominating Your Market

Another advantage of going an inch wide and a mile deep is that you can totally dominate the space you're in. You can own your niche. All your competitors are generalists—they don't know your business to the level that you do. They may know X, Y, and Z but you know Z inside and out, backwards and forwards. You can run circles around them with respect to Z.

Yes, your potential market is smaller, but that's by design. And by focusing your efforts on your niche, you gain a number of advantages:

- **Claim market ownership faster.** By focusing your product offerings, you can more quickly know all you need to know about your niche. Because your focus is so specific, so narrow, your learning curve is steep but shorter.

- **Less competition.** Since most companies go broad and shallow, your narrow and deep approach will set you apart. You can avoid going head-to-head with competitors by choosing one specific focus. Sure, your fellow pool suppliers may sell everything under the sun, from patio umbrellas to alarms to skimmers, but by zeroing in on salt water commercial pools, such as in physical therapy facilities, athletic clubs, and country clubs, you've separated yourself from the pack. In contrast to you, your competitors know next to nothing. You'll also be able to provide vastly superior customer service – another differentiator.

- **Optimized SEO.** Zeroing in on a limited number of keywords related to your business makes it easier to rank higher in Google when you combine SEO techniques with keyword rich content.

- **Faster market education.** Marketing to a targeted set of potential customers is much easier than trying to reach a vast and broad population. Customers with common needs and interests frequently share recommendations and "finds" with others like them, helping to build awareness and familiarity at a much faster pace.

## Finding Your Sweet Spot

If you're currently running a generalist business and you want to transition to a niche strategy, there are two key steps:

1. External analysis. Where are the opportunities in the market? What do customers want that they can't find, or that the

competition isn't currently providing? What are problems that your products or services could address?

2. Internal analysis. What are your strengths as a business that could be applied to address the existing market opportunities? What do you do well? What are you known for? What would you need to do to dominate the market?

## How Large is Your Niche?

Once you identify potential market niches, before you go all in, take a little time to research the size of those potential niches. I'm not saying you need to spend days and days and conduct sophisticated statistical analyses—don't go that far—but do enough that you feel confident that investing in that specialty will be worth your time and effort. Confirm that there are enough customers in that niche to be profitable for your business.

Let's take insurance, for example. A generalist strategy would be to offer life, home, and auto coverage like the 386,319 other agents, according to the Bureau of Labor Statistics. Everyone with a car needs auto insurance, so the market is huge. In fact, there were 268.8 million cars needing insurance as of 2016. So what are some untapped niche insurance markets?

Turns out equine insurance is a large and growing market. Only 17 percent of the 6 million horses in the U.S. are insured, reported *Insurance Journal* a number of years ago. Establishing yourself as a preeminent equine insurance provider would be much easier to do than trying to break into the market for, say, auto insurance. It would be much harder to get noticed in such a crowded field.

*We live in an age of specialists—a time when expertise is highly prized.*

## Packaging and Positioning Your Enterprise

Fortunately for you, I have cracked the formula on how to pick your niche effectively and quickly. Answer these questions for your business to determine your niche:

- **Who you are.** (What is your value proposition; everything rolls up to your value proposition)
- **What you do.** (What are your core products and services?)
- **Why you do it.** (What is your purpose? This will fuel and energize your culture.)
- **Why people want it.** (It's the best? It's the cheapest? Why do they buy?)
- **What makes you unique?** (Is it your process? Your service? Your materials? What?)
- **Who you do it for.** (Who is your target audience?)
- **What proof do you have to be the market leader?** (Can you provide case studies, testimonials, reviews, and other proof of performance?)
- **What will you look and sound like?** (What kind of slogan and messaging will you use to support ownership of this niche?)

Once you've settled on your niche, the next step is to make sure your internal and external processes are aligned.

Internally, you want to be sure that your operational processes make it easier to give your customers exactly what they're looking for in a timely manner. You'll also want to design materials that support your company's goal of dominating your market niche.

Packaging and positioning is vital. You have to know how to package and position your offering and service. Companies that do it well win. Period. Your business will never scale if you don't do this well.

If you can answer all of these questions, you'll be armed to effectively sell your product or service in the marketplace.

Don't try and bullshit here. It has to be real and authentic and deliverable.

Externally, there are many opportunities to position your business as the leading provider of your product or service. Using the following tools you can stake your claim and shape your reputation:

- Company website
- Blog
- Logo
- Stationery
- Direct mail materials
- Advertisements
- Social media posts

Everything you do to connect and communicate with prospects and customers impacts your market position—it affects how your company is perceived by your target market.

**Speed Read**

- By dominating your market you will: 1) Claim market ownership faster 2) Have less competition 3) Rank higher in Google 4) Educate your market faster.
- Here's how to effectively package and position your business in the marketplace: 1) Who you are 2) What you do 3) Why you do it 4) Why people want it 5) What makes you unique 6) Who you do it for 7) What proof do you have to be the market leader 8) What will you look and sound like?
- Position your company as the market leader—the expert in your niche—through your customer-facing marketing tools

like your website, blog, and social media, as well as internal processes and tools that support your superior product and service delivery.

# Competitive Intelligence

I f you aren't paying attention to your competition, you'll be out of business soon. You need to know who your competition is and how they operate in order to avoid major problems. Gathering competitive intelligence is a critical business task.

And don't tell me you don't have any competition—I assure you, you do. Some are direct competitors that sell the same products or services and others are indirect, selling products or services that are used by your target market instead of what you offer. For example, you may think that competitors for your management consulting firm consist only of other management consultants, when there are indirect competitors like websites that provide market research or freelance marketplaces that connect companies with subject-matter experts, to name just a couple.

Now, I'm not saying you should be so focused on your competition that you take your eyes off your own business and industry, but you do need to be aware of what your competitors are up to in order to get out and stay out in front. You can make smart decisions regarding R&D, new product development, branding, pricing, and promotions when you are crystal clear about where your business fits in the competitive landscape. Without that knowledge, you're operating blind, unaware of how you stack up and where the opportunities are.

Of course, one of the advantages of going an inch wide and a mile deep is that you won't be going head-to-head with many competitors. Your niche is one way you can differentiate yourself from all the other businesses in your space. But rarely are you the one and only business serving your target market.

## Conducting a SWOT Analysis

The best place to start in conducting competitive intelligence is understanding who you are and how you measure up to your competition. The only way to really do that is to assess your strengths, weaknesses, opportunities, and threats (SWOT). It's a process that helps you uncover what assets you can leverage and where you may be able to make headway in the marketplace.

You start by analyzing each factor in order to start formulating a plan for domination. This isn't meant to be an in-depth evaluation that lasts weeks—more like a down-and-dirty assessment. Be honest with yourself. Where does your business fall on each point?

**Strengths**. Your company's strengths are what set it apart from the competition. Where do you have an advantage? These might include things like:

- Low costs
- Unique product features
- Management experience

- Industry reputation
- Customer base

Strengths are potential advantages you can exploit that are due to internal operations.

**Weaknesses.** Likewise, weaknesses are also internal factors. They are the aspects of your business that are currently inferior to your competition. They are where competitors can beat you when you go head-to-head for a customer's business. Weaknesses can include things like:

- Lack of access to capital
- Long shipment lead times for inventory
- No online sales
- High employee turnover
- Remote geographic location

Weaknesses are the aspects of your business you want to downplay or that need to be addressed in order to win more business.

**Opportunities.** An opportunity is an external factor that your business can leverage to your advantage, such as new legislation that drives your product costs down or a new market for your technology that is emerging. Opportunities can include:

- Vocal customer advocates
- An emerging market for your services
- New legislation
- Positive media coverage
- Chance to partner with local resources

Since they are external to your business, opportunities aren't situations you can necessarily control, but they are chances for you to gain a competitive advantage.

**Threats.** Where opportunities are factors that can benefit a company, threats are external factors that can harm it. These, too, are situations no one business can impact, but that they need to strategize how to avoid or lessen the damage. Threats can include:

- Natural disasters
- Decline in demand
- Increasing competition
- Rising raw material costs
- Changes in the industry

Overall, threats are obstacles to your company's success, whether due to shifts in the economy, your market or industry, or some other outside force. While you typically can't stop or prevent the threat, you can certainly take steps to mitigate their impact.

### Using the Competition's Weaknesses to Showcase Your Strengths

In all of my businesses, I always took every opportunity to study the competition and identify where they were weak. That way, I could shine a bright spotlight on those faults whenever we went head-to-head for new business. I'm sure this strategy is what won us the million-dollar national oil and lubricant account a few years ago.

The oil and lubricant retailer had decided to invest $1 million in developing an entirely new website that would be designed to do a better job of supporting its franchisees, driving traffic to local offices, and using digital promotional tools to attract new customers.

The assignment was to pitch a creative approach that would achieve these objectives.

The first thing my team and I did was review the list of all the agencies competing for the work. I saw immediately that there was no way our 120-person agency could successfully compete with major ad agencies with 5,000 employees. If we tried, we would certainly lose. I had to uncover what their weaknesses were for us to have a shot at all.

Turns out, where they were weak we were strong—on data analytics. We were a nimble data-focused firm while the big firms were all about creative and didn't really understand the data. That was our "in."

We obtained access to the company's Google Analytics and spent weeks poring over the numbers. Then we created a pitch that brought that data to life, explaining who their customers were, when they would be most likely to come into an oil and lubricant location, and how best to entice them. We arrived at the pitch with a huge 6' by 4'4" board with graphics demonstrating what we learned about their customer's journey. On-hand to answer questions were three data analysts, not the creative director that all the other companies had leading their teams.

We zeroed in on the data we knew no one else could decipher and explained the features the site needed to have. Although we had been told we "had" to bring creative concepts to present, we changed the rules and brought what we knew would make us stand out from the crowd. We told management, "Now that we know this, we can get to work on a creative strategy for you. But without this analysis, any creative proposal would be ineffective."

With that, we highlighted what our competition couldn't provide—accurate data analysis—and won the account. We fought on the battlefield we knew, where we were strong, rather than getting dragged into trying to compete on a front we would certainly lose—creative.

That's the power of competitive intelligence. If you don't have it, you'll lose.

Studying your competition is a smart way to lessen external threats and strategize how to take advantage of opportunities by leveraging your strengths and downplaying your company's weaknesses.

*You can make smart decisions regarding R&D, new product development, branding, pricing, and promotions when you are crystal clear about where your business fits in the competitive landscape.*

## Conducting Competitive Assessments

Once you know your own business's market position through the SWOT analysis you just completed, it's time to turn your attention to your competition. Becoming informed about the competitive landscape helps you make better, faster decisions that contribute to your bottom line. Ignore your competition and they will shut you down.

Start by conducting a SWOT analysis on each of your major competitors, just as you did for your own business. Think through what you perceive to be their strengths, weaknesses, opportunities, and threats. This step helps ensure that your perspective is accurate. You may *think* you're stronger on some aspects, but once you really dig into all the data, you may get a reality check that will provide a path to success.

Next, identify what you can do to gain the advantage—how can you magnify their weaknesses and mitigate their strengths?

## Setting Up a Competitive Intelligence System

After you've finished your initial SWOT analysis of each competitor, create a way to monitor their practices on an ongoing basis. The assessment you've done is only good for the short-term—as soon as market conditions shift, it will be out of date. To get ahead of your competitors, invest in competitive research tools that will offer ongoing observations and insights about their decisions and actions.

Some of the benefits of competitive research include:

- More accurate forecasting figures
- Keeping tabs on competitor pricing
- Improved target marketing
- Awareness of the latest competing products and services
- Identifying new potential markets

While you'll want to stay informed about all aspects of a company's operations, your main focus should be on marketing information. Get inside their heads and dissect their marketing tactics to one-up them and be able to anticipate future tactics.

Here are some of the best tools on the market you'll want to invest in—several are tools my digital marketing agency used to gain the edge:

**Google Alert**. This feature within Google allows you to create search terms, such as the names of all of your competitors, which will then trigger email alerts to be sent whenever those names, or other industry terms you specify, appear in news reports or online portals. Free.

**SimilarWeb**. Even with the free version of SimilarWeb, you can gather a ton of information about your competition's online operations. From analyzing their online marketing strategy and comparing it to yours, to comparing traffic stats, sources of traffic, referring websites, as well as organic and paid keyword reports, SimilarWeb provides quantitative data to help you spot ways to mimic and even surpass their online marketing efforts without breaking the bank. Free version and paid.

**SpyFu**. To get even more detail regarding your competitors' most profitable keywords, you'll want to turn to SpyFu, which will deliver information on more profitable keywords you can use. You can also see how much their keywords overlap with yours. Paid.

**RankSignals.** Another useful piece of data to gather is where your competition's backlinks are coming from. RankSignals will hand over your competitors' backlinks and best traffic sources. Paid.

**SEMrush.** Another great tool for checking out the competition's organic keywords, keyword ranking position, and search volume for the keywords they're relying on is SEMrush. Paid.

**BuzzSumo.** This is more of a social media tool than advertising or keyword device, but BuzzSumo shows you what the most-shared content is for a particular keyword or topic. You can then devise an editorial calendar for future posts that increases the likelihood that your posts will also be shared far and wide. Paid.

These tools can help you boost traffic to your site, build brand awareness, and ultimately increase your total revenue.

## Brick and Mortar Research

One of the best ways to assess how your competitors deliver on their promises is to shop them yourself—play the role of a customer and see how they perform. Walk into their retail store, sit down in their restaurant, ask for a free consultation, or call for customer support. How would you grade their performance?

If you don't feel comfortable walking into the competition's offices or fear you'll be recognized if you do, there are a few ways you can try and get a sense of what they're like to do business with:

**Hire a secret shopper.** If you're in the retail industry, I'm sure you're familiar with mystery shoppers or secret shoppers. These are companies that hire people to shop and write up evaluations of their experiences. Many companies hire mystery shoppers to assess their own operations but you can also study your competition this way.

**Pick up printed materials.** Take every opportunity to pick up marketing materials from your competitors. You can try requesting them online as well as grabbing them as you walk by their booth at a trade show or conference. Don't lie to get it, but take it when it's available.

**Ask your customers for their feedback.** Find customers who have had experience buying from your competitors and ask for their honest breakdown of the pros and cons of dealing with them versus your business. Where are they strong? What do they do better than you? What didn't the customer like? Offer an incentive for their time and input.

**Study online reviews.** Scan the reviews companies have received from their customers to better understand where they're falling short. Did they not follow up? Were they rude? What words did customers use to describe the experience? Check out Google and Yelp and any sites where the company's products are sold to see what real customers have to say.

### Incorporating Best Practices

To gain a competitive advantage, you'll want to study and apply the best processes, strategies, and tactics your competition is using. To start, you need to determine what your industry's best practices are and which organizations demonstrate them. Then copy them—cherry pick the best practices within multiple competitors and introduce them into your operations.

### Speed Read

- Benefits of competitive research include: 1) More accurate forecasting figures 2) Keeping tabs on competitor pricing 3) Improved target marketing 4) Awareness of the latest competing products and services 5) Identifying new potential markets
- Online competitive research tools include: 1) Google Alert 2) SimilarWeb 3) SpyFu 4) RankSignals 5) SEMrush 6) BuzzSumo.

- Offline research tools include: 1) Hire a secret shopper 2) Pick up printed materials 3) Ask your customers for their feedback 4) Study online reviews.

# Develop a Recurring Revenue Stream

Without recurring revenue you don't have a business. Recurring revenue allows you to have stability and predictability and provides the ability to scale. If you don't have recurring revenue, you're project-based. Every day is a new day. You start over every morning hoping that you can replicate yesterday's revenue. That's a dangerous place to be.

If you ever want a shot at creating serious wealth and selling your business, the only way you can do that is with recurring revenue. End of story.

We all know what revenue, or income, is, but I suspect the concept of recurring revenue may be unfamiliar to some of you. It was certainly not something I had ever heard of or thought of when I started my first business.

Recurring revenue, according to Webster's, is "happening time and again"—it's revenue that is generated on a regular basis, such as every week, every month, or every quarter. As a buyer, recurring revenue is those monthly fees you pay for cell phone service, access to your country club, or identity fraud insurance, versus the one-time payment for the purchase of equipment, fine art, business trips or logo design, for example. Recurring revenue is generated as long as the client is obligated to pay it, such as through a contract, or for as long as the client desires access to the product or service connected to that monthly payment.

From a business perspective, recurring revenue is key to exponential growth. To scale with speed, you need to be consistently adding incremental revenue each month—using your existing revenue stream as a base on which to expand. You can't do that if you're selling one-time products or services. Believe me, I learned that the hard way.

When I started my first business, I sold web design and development to small businesses in the town where I was going to college. I typically sold six to eight sites a month at an average cost of $10,000 each. Each month we'd generate $60,000-80,000, which was great money. However, as soon as a project was done, I had to sell another website to a new client to maintain that level of revenue.

As the business grew, we hired more people, moved into bigger space, and took on larger financial responsibilities. The knowledge that one slow month could put us in a bad financial position was nerve-wracking. Eventually, it led to the company's collapse. We couldn't keep up with our costs.

No matter how many websites I sold, growing the business seemed to get harder. That's because I had created a lifestyle business without realizing it.

Websites are one-time projects. Clients hired us, paid us, we did the work, and in order to earn more revenue, I had to sell more websites to more clients. It was a hamster wheel. Eventually I realized that we couldn't succeed without finding a recurring source of revenue. I did, but I had to shut down the website company in order to do it. One-off engagements are nearly impossible to scale.

To be successful—to scale with speed—you need to base your business on a recurring source of revenue, not one-time projects.

Let me explain what I mean by comparing how my company operated with one-off sales versus how we could have grown with recurring revenue.

**Project-based revenue**. Let's say the business earned, to keep the numbers simple, $100,000 a month. After two years, we would have earned a total of $1.2 million x 2 years, or $2.4 million. That's how much money had flowed through the company.

**Recurring revenue**. Now if we had added a recurring source of revenue, such as an ongoing package of maintenance, SEO, and online marketing for which we charged clients $2,000/month, let's see how the numbers would be different. We would still earn $100,000/month from website design, which is $2.4 million over two years, but add to that $2,000 per 8 clients, or $16,000 per month. Each month we'd add 8 more clients, or $16,000. So after 24 months, we would have earned $2.4 million in flat fees from clients plus $1,248,000 in the first year from recurring revenue, and an additional $3,552,000 in year two. That's an additional $4,800,000 over two years from recurring revenue alone.

And the numbers keep rising from there with each new client added. That's the power of recurring revenue.

It was also my takeaway from closing that business down. It was a hard lesson but one that I applied from there on out. All of my businesses from then on had a recurring revenue component.

## Rising Popularity

Businesses seem to be realizing this, as we've seen a number of industries evolve into leveraging recurring revenue. Research conducted by Aria

Systems reported that 46.7 percent of all businesses in the U.S. have or are developing recurring revenue channels. Some industries seem to have made the switch while others either are oblivious or are unsure of how to convert one-time payments into recurring revenue models.

Software as a service (SaaS) is certainly one of the most prominent examples of a shift to a recurring revenue model. Where customers used to buy an off-the-shelf software product like Microsoft Office or TurboTax at a retail store for a couple hundred bucks every year, software marketers have shifted to a monthly payment for as long as you want to be able to use the software. In exchange, you're assured that you'll always have access to the most up-to-date version of the program you're using. That's recurring revenue—a monthly payment for continued customer access with no end in sight.

While SaaS is the new model in the software industry, there are a number of opportunities to convert your one-time purchase into recurring revenue, or to create an entirely new income stream.

*Recurring revenue is key to exponential growth.*

## Five Recurring Revenue Models

One of the reasons recurring revenue models are becoming more common is that customers typically prefer them, Aria Systems found, reporting that "customers prefer to 'pay as they go' in small increments." The ability to spread a purchase price out over time, rather than having to come up with a large upfront payment is appealing. It's why auto leasing is such a big industry, for example. Many customers would rather pay monthly for use of the make and model car they desire, trading them in every two to three years for the latest model, instead of having to put down thousands of dollars to purchase something outright.

But leasing isn't the only recurring revenue model. Depending on your product or service, you may find one of these five models is a fit for your company:

**Retainer.** Common in the marketing and legal world, retainer agreements involve having the customer pay a monthly fee for guaranteed access to your professional skills. Some firms, such as public relations agencies, charge a set amount for an agreed-upon number of hours to be devoted to your company, which is paid whether all of those hours are used or not.

Others take a deposit and work off of that amount until the balance is zero, at which point they require another deposit in advance of additional work being done. Many virtual assistants operate using this model.

Do you offer a service that your customers could use on a regular basis? SEO updates or cybersecurity monitoring, for example, could be converted to retainer arrangements. Transcription, carpet cleaning, lawn care, and child care could also potentially be sold as an ongoing revenue stream.

**Subscription.** Newspapers and magazines were the dominant industries using the subscription business model, but today you can sell a subscription to a wide variety of products and services. Today, customers can buy subscriptions to everything from razors to clothing to beauty supplies, snacks, contact lenses, and even furnace filters.

Amazon has gotten into the game, offering subscriptions to common pantry items, from paper products to food to health and beauty products.

But subscriptions don't have to be limited to products. You can even bundle services. Designpickle offers unlimited graphic design services for a low monthly price of $370 or an annual price of $3,552.

Similarly, photographers could sell annual subscriptions to their services that provide a monthly photo session for a new baby through age one. Or a dry cleaner could offer a subscription for five dress shirts cleaned per week for one low price.

What product or service do you sell that customers may want ongoing access to? If you're a retailer, can you sell a subscription to, say, the latest jewelry item or stationery line your store stocks? If you run a font foundry, how about a subscription to the latest typeface your team has developed? Of if you sell printer ink, how about a subscription to ensure your customers never see that "low ink" warning on their monitor?

**Contract revenue.** Any product or service that requires that customers sign an agreement that locks them in for a certain period of time, typically annually, provides contract revenue. For example, if you contract with a janitorial service to clean up after your crew three nights a week, you'll be asked to commit to a certain length of service, such as six or twelve months. It's the same with leasing office space—you have to commit to remaining in the office for a certain period of time, often 3-5 years, or you'll have to pay an early termination fee.

The reasoning behind requiring a contract is frequently because there is set up work that needs to be done that costs the company money up front. The janitorial service, for example, needs to learn what you want cleaned and how at the start—there's a learning curve. Or with office space, the landlord may need to make some modifications for you—moving walls, replacing carpeting, adding lighting—that will cost some money. Those investments only make sense if you, the tenant, are willing to continuing leasing for longer than a year.

Is there a product or service you could offer clients that could be provided over time but that might require some initial set up work?

**Service plans.** Even if you run a product-based business, you may be able to create a new income stream by adding a service offering. Do the products you sell require infrequent maintenance?

How about offering your customers the option to pay in advance for a service plan?

Universal Imports of Rochester, New York, is an automotive repair shop and luxury used car dealership that created the Universal Imports Car Care Club several years ago to give customers a reason to come back in more frequently. For $39/year, customers who join the club receive a free inspection, discounted parts and labor on work they do have done, discounted oil changes, as well as free regular check-ups. Each time a customer stops in for an inspection or service, Universal Imports has the opportunity to offer repair work the client may not have realized they needed. It's a win-win.

HVAC companies often sell annual maintenance programs for new furnaces or air conditioning units they install, to reduce the odds of an emergency and allay customer's fears of being inconvenienced.

Computer consultants could sell ongoing malware protection or assessments. Inground pool installers could sell annual opening and closing plans. Car washes could, and do, offer unlimited washes in exchange for a monthly fee.

What do you sell that customers might want to protect with a maintenance or service plan?

**Membership**. Businesses based on a membership model, whether online or off, require a regular payment—usually monthly—to remain part of the community. Online membership programs have become extremely popular in the last couple of years as consultants, coaches, and service providers have created online spaces for people to congregate, network, and learn from one another.

Some membership programs, such as Jason T. Smith's Secret Beach, charge monthly or on annual basis for access to information about reselling on eBay and Amazon. As long as the buyer pays the monthly fee, they remain a member of the group but as soon as they cancel, they have no more access to the training and information sharing within the group.

Today you can find membership models such as the paid version of SurveyMonkey, which requires a monthly fee to design, distribute, and analyze online surveys. Or Spotify, which, for a monthly fee of around $10, provides you with access to millions of songs you can play through your smartphone. Or there is the Jelly of the Month club type offerings which Clark Griswold made famous in "National Lampoon's Christmas Vacation."

If your product or service offering requires an ongoing monthly or annual payment to access, you've built a membership business.

Recurring revenue is essential for scaling quickly, but on a more basic level, it evens out cash flow and reduces the risk of financial shortfalls. You must have recurring revenue if you want to quickly scale up.

## Speed Read

- Recurring revenue is an ongoing stream of income, rather than a one-time payment for goods or services.
- The 5 types of recurring revenue business models are: 1) Retainer 2) Subscription 3) Contract revenue 4) Service plans 5) Membership.
- Without recurring revenue you will never be able to sell your company and gain full financial freedom.
- By building a solid base of recurring revenue, you can focus on continuously adding to that base, rather than having to start from zero each month with respect to accounts receivable.

# Validate Your Service or Product

Taking massive action quickly is the name of the game if you're after major success. Whether you run an existing business or are just starting out, it's critical to confirm there is a market for what you're selling. Startups needs to confirm in advance that the market wants what they're selling and existing businesses need to reinvent themselves every six months, to stay current with what customers want.

You've heard the adage "Ready. Aim. Fire," right? That's the best way to line up a shot. Taking action without validating your idea or approach is the equivalent of "Ready. Fire. Aim." Not as effective. At all. In fact, you can lose your shirt investing money in a venture that is doomed from the start.

Fortunately, there are ways to do some market research before you roll out your new product, service, or business, to confirm that you're on the right track and can be profitable. There's no point in investing in something that has little chance of success. That's what I want to help you avoid. Because it *is* avoidable.

## Testing the Waters

Before you move ahead full throttle, test your concept, test your marketing, test your packaging—test every aspect of your new product or service. Since your business is built on a particular market niche or set of products, focus your testing on what your company will specialize in. Asking potential customers if they would buy from a business that sells X is too vague, so drill down to your products and services to get some useful answers.

You'll want to get feedback on:

- Product or service features
- Pricing
- Packaging
- Positioning

Of course, the more feedback you can get, the better. But even small numbers of responses to informal market research are useful. In fact, to be statistically significant—meaning the result reflects the market as a whole—100 responses are often enough. According to market research firm driveresearch, "the minimum is 100 completes [meaning the survey has been completed], 400 completes is the gold standard, and 1,000 completes is ideal if the same and budget allow your organization to pursue."

More precisely, there is a formula you can use to determine how confident you can be in the results. And the number of research responses you need depends on the group you're researching.

Here is the exact formula, compliments of the National Business Research Institute, to determine how many people you need to hear from for your results to be valid: https://www.nbrii.com/our-process/ sample-size-calculator. For example, if you assume a potential market of at least 20,000 people and a market research sample of about 100 people, you would have a 95 percent confidence level that the results are significant. That's not many and should be fairly easy to get.

We came out with a new marketing service that we wanted to validate to be sure it would be profitable. That service was A-B testing. We approached eight clients that we knew could benefit from the new service and would be receptive to trying it. We identified opportunities on their website to improve. We quickly saw the yield, which validated the need, desire, and want for the service and helped us price at a premium based on the value we were providing.

## Conduct Market Research

If you're worried that you won't be able to find enough people to interview as part of your research, don't be. There are several online market research tools that can help you assess whether you have a viable business or offering. Here are several you should check out:

### Primary Research—Conducting Your Own Studies

FocusGroupIt. This market research platform runs focus groups (you bring together groups of people online to discuss and share their opinions on your product or service concept or features). It enables you to gather qualitative feedback online using easy-to-use systems. You can sign up for a free account with limited options and upgrade your plan if needed; monthly costs start at $49.

GutCheck. Conduct qualitative research on everything from product concept to flavor to pricing, packing, names, and more with the help of the researchers here. Draft questions and get responses through this paid site.

Loop11. This website usability testing tool allows you to test your site or that of competitors to see what you need to do to improve results. Pricing starts at $49/month.

SurveyMonkey. This online tool for creating and sharing surveys has a free version as well as a premium version for more features and sample sizes. Easy to use and share, this is an excellent resource for designing surveys.

User Interviews. This research platform connects companies looking for user experience feedback with participants willing to test things like websites, products, and different variations of product features. Companies can conduct one-on-one interviews, host focus groups, or send out questionnaires via the platform.

If you're familiar with how to run focus groups, you could also use Google Hangouts as a focus group platform to bring together participants yourself.

While primary research is the way to go to gather feedback on your ideas and plans, if you're looking for existing data about things like the size of your market, consumer trends, or how your website performs, there are sources of secondary research you can turn to.

### Secondary Research—Referring to Data Others Have Collected

American Fact Finder. This free resource for searching U.S. Census data makes it easy to track down existing facts about U.S. consumers, households, and businesses.

Think With Google. Another free resource, this one from Google has useful data about consumer trends, including how consumer behavior changes with seasons, holidays, and other special events.

Research is important because it's a stepping stone to action. You don't want to get so hung up on research that you don't ship it—you don't ever move forward. But routinely stopping to pressure test ideas allows you to quickly scale without making huge mistakes. Sure, you'll make mistakes along the way, but ideally they'll be minor and inexpensive.

*Validating your business isn't about proving that you were right, it's about finding a business offering that customers are willing to pay you for that leverages your strengths and expertise.*

## Avoid Scaling with a Bad Idea

Every once in a while comes a story of a company that failed on a major scale due to poor testing and validation. This is what I don't want to happen to you.

Take Juicero. Maybe you've heard of it.

Juicero was a $700 juice machine that tried to piggyback on the huge success of the Keurig machine (dubbed the "Keurig for juice"), which revolutionized coffee drinking by placing coffee into single-serve cups. Like Keurig, the Juicero was a high-end machine designed to tap into the growing juicing trend. The machine allowed users to make their own healthy juices at home. Explains a CIO article, "Users just had to plug in pre-sold packets of diced juice and vegetables into the machine and then it produces juice."

Sounds great, right? Convenient and healthy all in one.

The company had started raising venture capital in 2013 but didn't actually release the product until 2016. And then a 2017 Bloomberg article was published that revealed the machine wasn't as useful as advertised. In fact, a Bloomberg reporter had done a head-to-head test with the Juicero machine, timing how long it took to squeeze the juice packets by hand versus through the machine. The reporter won. It was simpler and faster just to squeeze the juice packets by hand, without the use of the expensive machine.

It wasn't long after this exposé that Juicero shut down, in September 2017. It's likely the company never considered speed of delivery when testing its machine.

The *New York Times'* David Gelles summed up the Juicero situation, saying, "The company sold a $700 wi-fi-enabled juicer, trying to solve a problem that did not exist."

In my world of digital marketing, the failures we experienced were typically because our clients got too hung up on using marketing-speak to describe their product or features. In designing their websites, clients would insist on using descriptive words that were frequently used internally, rather than polling customers to learn what words and phrases *they* would use when searching for a product like it.

For example, instead of using a keyword like "car" the company might use "vehicle" or "auto" on its website and then wonder why they had no traffic. Or instead of "consultant" they might use words like "counselor," "advisor," or "problem-solver." Yes, those words are synonyms but they're not words most customers would search for online.

Before investing money in your marketing, ask your target market for input.

## Pivot, If Necessary

If entrepreneurs Bob Saris, Basel Fakhoury, and Dennis Meng had done that up front, they could have saved themselves months of time and energy invested in a service no one wanted.

The men spent a year working on a mobile app that would provide travelers with 24/7 access to upscale hotel concierge services. Excited, they launched it and only then discovered that they didn't have a market. No one was using it.

Frantic, they started gathering user data to try and understand what was going on. They even bought refundable plane tickets to able to enter airports and sit in the gates talking to potential customers. After hundreds of these types of traveler interviews, the three were forced to accept that they had a dud of a business.

"If we had talked to them earlier, we would have known much sooner that our app wasn't going to be successful," they admitted in an *Inc.* article.

What they did recognize was that they could help companies gather feedback from customers, so they pivoted and formed User Interviews, the automated platform for recruiting and scheduling market research studies and product tests I mentioned above.

> "I once heard someone describe running a startup as riding a bike while building it," said Meng. "That description couldn't have been more accurate for us. Before we even had a website, we had companies trying to pay us for our services. We had dozens of paying clients before the first version of our technology platform was complete."

User Interviews is successful because the founders were willing to assess what they had and rework their business model based on customer feedback and market research into what holes existed in the marketplace. They pivoted once in possession of market data.

### Four Steps to Validation

To simplify the process of testing and validating your idea, let me share the four main steps you need to use to confirm you have a viable product, service, or business.

1. **Pick a market research tool**. Find a quick, cost-effective sample size of your target market to validate there is a need for your idea. Confirm customers want the features you plan to include

or like the packaging you've designed. Test your proposed price. Even if they like the price, can you make money at that figure?

2. **Conduct online research**. Go online to get feedback from a subset of your target market. Start selling your offering and pay attention to the feedback you get. Are they handing over their money 10 out of 10 times or are customers reluctant to pay for what you're promoting.

3. **Adjust your offering based on the feedback you've received**. Are there features no one wants? Other features they do that you hadn't thought about including?

4. **Bring a soft opening to market**. Many new businesses announce a big grand opening weeks or months after they officially open for business, giving the venture time to test customer reaction to what they're selling. Some use the pre-grand opening time to "get the bugs out," while others end up doing a major shift or pivot if real-time feedback points clearly in another direction.

Although you may have invested a substantial amount of resources in creating and building your business or new product, to be successful you must be willing to change your mind if your customers give you feedback that suggests a better approach. Validating your business isn't about proving that you were right, it's about finding a business offering that customers are willing to pay you for that leverages your strengths and expertise.

### Speed Read

- To test the waters, get feedback on: 1) Product or service features 2) Pricing 3) Packaging 4) Positioning
- Use these four market research tools as part of your validation process: 1) FocusGroupIt 2) GutCheck 3) Loop11 4) SurveyMonkey.

- The four steps to validation are: 1) Pick a market research tool 2) Conduct online research 3) Adjust your offering based on the feedback you've received 4) Bring a soft opening to market.
- Existing businesses should be reinventing themselves as it relates to their products and services and then validating them to stay relevant.

**Part 3**

# Execute with Speed: The Process

*"Speed wins the race."*
**– Judge Graham**

Once you've got the basic foundation in place for scaling your business effectively, it's time to shift your attention to doing it with speed. Being able to move nimbly and quickly can provide an unbeatable competitive advantage. If you can move fast, you can get ahead of the competition and stay there.

To grow with speed, you must be able to execute quickly. That means gathering just enough information to allow you to make an informed decision and then deciding. There's no time for hemming and hawing—just go.

You also need to infuse that sense of urgency throughout all ranks of your organization, so everyone understands the importance of getting things done immediately. There's no time to waste.

Following a one-page attack and conquer plan you devise as a guide to business growth, you can push your business forward and make things happen in a fraction of the time it takes everyone else.

Simplifying your internal processes to fuel your momentum and eliminate any roadblocks also helps you scale with speed.

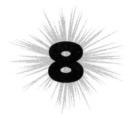

# The Power of Starting Now

Now that you've made a decision, it's time to take action. Immediately.

The key here is not to get bogged down in too much planning and tracking and evaluating. Sure, those are important, but to scale with speed you need to jumpstart your progress and create momentum. The only way to make that happen is to do something—almost anything—right now.

## List Your Priorities

Yes, there are 1 million things you need to do, could do, right now. But what is the one thing that, if you did it, would make the most difference in your business today?

Make a list of your top priorities—no more than four for now. Then choose one and go. Get it done.

Pick one of the low-hanging fruit or the easiest-to-finish tasks to make some quick progress.

Maybe that task is calling a hot lead that came in yesterday to schedule an appointment. Or maybe it's following up on the bid you submitted last month, or calling the contact person for a proposal you want to submit but can't because you're missing one piece of data. Maybe it's calling your webmaster to talk about how to update your website, or emailing your human resource director about posting a job opening; or maybe it's taking the first step to let a low performer go.

Honestly, it doesn't matter which of the four top priorities you start with as long as you start. Just do it. Get it done.

### The 75/25 Approach

I came up with the 75/25 rule out of sheer necessity.

A few years ago, I was so stressed at work I wasn't sure where my time was going. I would look up at the clock and discover I'd been at work for 12 hours, but it felt like I hadn't accomplished anything. I was always scrambling. I frequently didn't know how I was going to cover payroll *and* pay myself.

So one day I stopped to try and figure out what I was doing wrong. I mapped out a typical day and immediately saw the problem. I was spending more than 75 percent of my day on non-revenue-generating activities. That was my problem. I needed to shift where I was investing my time and set higher targets for myself.

That's when I came up with the 75/25 approach, which I laid out on a form I developed called the Money Sheet (See JudgeGraham. com for your copy). The Money Sheet contains your top six to eight priorities that you *have* to complete that day in order to hit your monthly revenue targets.

But just listing your priorities does nothing for you. Once you've identified what you need to do, you have to actually take action. Do something.

I learned to split my priorities between two major types of activities—revenue-generating and administrative—to ensure that the business continues to function even while I'm focused on building it. I call it the 75/25 approach to task completion.

Once I put a task on my Money Sheet, I committed to getting it done that day, no matter how seemingly insurmountable the task was.

First, I identify six to eight priorities related to generating revenue. I'm going to spend 75 percent of my time on those tasks each day. These might include checking in with each member of my sales team, preparing new business proposals, following up with leads, calling key clients to ask about upcoming opportunities. If I work a standard eight-hour day (which I never do, honestly, because I love what I do), six hours of that day is going to be spent on generating revenue.

Then I identify two to three priorities related to managing the business that need to be completed each day, such as calling in payroll, scheduling a meeting with my accountant about taxes, or setting up performance reviews. These aren't revenue-generating activities but they still need to be done to be successful. I plan to spend 25 percent of my day, or two out of eight hours, on these administrative action items.

| 75% | 25% |
|---|---|
|  |  |
|  |  |
|  |  |
|  |  |
|  |  |

## Time is Money

We all want to be conscientious and do our best work consistently, but you need to weigh that need for quality with the time it will take.

According to Clio's 2017 Legal Trends Report, attorneys bill an average of 2.3 hours per day and spend six hours more on non-billable tasks, like scheduling, sending invoices, and technology glitches. That's the majority of their day!

Scoro's estimates are a little better, suggesting that workers are engaged in billable work 60 percent of the day. But still, 40 percent of their time is wasted on administrative tasks.

Don't let minor, inconsequential activities fill your day. Spending hours on social media, attending networking events several times a week, or constantly strategizing your next move is not going to get you where you want to go. You're wasting time, dragging your feet, and not setting yourself up to conquer anything.

The truth is, money likes speed. Money comes to those who take action quickly.

It's surprising what can happen when you move quickly to take advantage of an opportunity. I remember several years ago, when I was running a digital marketing agency, that I heard through the grapevine that a national consumer packaged goods company was looking for a new agency of record. That meant it would be a big contract worth potentially hundreds of thousands of dollars to the agency selected. Unfortunately, the company had already had initial meetings with several agencies and had narrowed the field to three by the time I got wind of the situation.

So what did I do? I started calling the chief marketing officer, who was also the co-owner, asking for the chance to be considered. I pestered her, calling three times the first day and leaving messages. I also sent her four emails explaining why we would be the perfect marketing partner. Then I had a big Edible Arrangement delivered to her with a note that pleaded with her to take my call. The next day when I dialed her number, she answered.

"I'm impressed with your persistence," she told me. "You're relentless."

I took that as a compliment.

Then, as I had explained in my phone messages and emails, I told her why our firm was the best choice for their marketing situation. She listened and then told me that they had scheduled the three finalist presentations for later in the week, so we would need to put together our best pitch and present it the following day. We had 24 hours to research, strategize, and pull together our best pitch.

My team and I pulled an all-nighter, did some great work, and were rewarded the next day when, following our pitch, the CMO told us, "I'm not even going to bring the other three firms in. The work is yours."

That contract was worth $1 million and we landed it within 48 hours of first hearing that the company was even looking.

That's the advantage of starting immediately—you uncover new opportunities and can go after them. Start now. Be relentless in your pursuit of the priorities you've set.

*Workers are engaged in billable work 60 percent of the day.*

## Pushing Past Fear

Sometimes we avoid a task because we're afraid of it. Either we're fearful because we don't know how to do it, or how to even begin, and other times we're nervous about what will happen if we do, in fact complete it.

Paralyzing fear creeps in and can make us freeze. The best way to get rid of that feeling of dread is to take action. Start executing. Not only will it reduce your stress level because your brain can be stressed and focused on achieving simultaneously, but you'll make progress toward your goals, which will generate dopamine—you'll feel better.

If you're uncomfortable making sales calls, do it anyway—promise yourself a reward if that will propel you forward. Pick up the phone, stumble through your pitch, and get better with each call you make. You learn something with every action you take, either through the feedback you receive or through the internal self-assessment we all take.

Doing anything, even the wrong thing, is better than doing nothing.

## Preventing Procrastination

Getting started is the hardest part, of course. Putting things off is so much easier in the short-term, but so disappointing in the long-term. Procrastination is the enemy of thinking bigger and conquering anything, really.

We come up with plenty of reasons why now isn't the right time to do something, or maybe why we don't really *have* to do something right now. Waiting until tomorrow, or "later," won't have any real impact, we tell ourselves.

And yet it does. Every delay holds you back. It prevents you from accomplishing what you set out to do.

So how can you stop procrastinating and make progress? Here are five steps to get you going now:

1. **Set a goal and be specific.** Do you want to double revenue in the next 12 months? Hit $5 million in sales? Land Facebook as a client? Move into new space? What are you working toward right now?

It's important to quantify your goal so that you can measure your progress. Instead of wanting to "increase sales," commit to a dollar figure. Rather than "adding employees," decide you want to employee 25 engineers by year-end.

Or maybe you want to earn your MBA. That's a great goal. All you need to do is assign a graduation date to quantify your objective and you're set.

2. **Break your goal down into steps.** I've heard of this process called "chunking" and it refers to identifying all the steps you'll go through to achieve your goal.

Make a list of each step you need to complete to reach your goal. Maybe there are four major tasks, or maybe there are 10. List all of them. Then break each of those tasks down into smaller tasks. Keep doing that—breaking down each step—until each task is 10-15 minutes long. You want individual tasks that are quick and simple to tackle. Sure, you may have a list of 200 such tasks, but they'll be much easier to complete when you know each one will only take you a few minutes.

3. **Harness your fear.** Imagine your worst-case scenario. Seriously. What's the absolute worst thing that could happen if you don't meet your goal?

Think about that.

Maybe your worst-case is feeling disappointed in yourself. Or maybe it's that your competitor captures such a large share of your market that you encounter sales resistance and have to shut down. Or perhaps something in between those two extremes—maybe you learned you're locked into your five-year lease, which severely limits your business growth because of your physical space.

Use those fears you've just identified to generate the adrenaline you need to take action right now. Remind yourself of what could happen if you continue to do nothing and procrastinate.

4. **Find a goal buddy.** We are 65 percent more likely to achieve a goal when we share it with someone else, according to the American Society of Training and Development (ASTD). It becomes a commitment and we don't want to let the other person down.

However, if we share our goal with someone else and then schedule an "accountability appointment" to check in, we increase our chances of success by 95 percent.

So find someone—a fellow business owner, a mentor, an advisor, or a friend—and tell that person what you're striving to do. Then set a lunch date or appointment during which you'll report on your progress. You could even put money on it, promising to reach a certain milestone or pay up a certain amount.

5. **Do something this instant.** Stop planning and chunking your goal and take some action right this minute. Pick up the phone, send an email, print out a form you need to complete, register for that conference you really need to attend—do anything.

Even small tasks completed create momentum. You do one thing and the next thing becomes that much easier to start and then finish. It's like a stone rolling down a hill—it might start slowly but the more distance it travels, the faster it goes. That's what you want. Momentum.

### The High of Accomplishment

When you finish something, your brain produces dopamine, a neurotransmitter that regulates the brain's reward and pleasure centers, explains *Psychology Today*. Dopamine produces pleasure that elevates your mood. The more you get done, the better you feel, thanks to dopamine, and the more you engage in pursuing new goals.

The more substantial your accomplishment, the more dopamine your brain releases.

As soon as you take steps toward your goal(s), the better you'll feel—literally—and the easier it will become to continue making progress.

So start now!

## Speed Read

- Start now, focusing 75 percent of your day on revenue-generating activities (visit JudgeGraham.com to get the Money Sheet to help you). Reduce the time you spend on administrative tasks that don't bring money in the door.
- Five steps to overcoming procrastination include: 1) Set a goal and be specific 2) Break your goal down into steps 3) Harness your fear 4) Find a goal buddy 5) Do something this instant.
- As soon as you list your six to eight top priorities, you must start taking action now. Don't wait.

# Make Decisions Quickly

I f you get nothing else from this book, I want you to learn how to start making decisions fast. Effective, world-class leaders understand the power of making quick decisions no matter what the stakes are. If you don't learn how to make decisions quickly your business will fail and you'll never scale with speed.

A core strength of mine is being able to make 15 decisions before a typical leader makes one or two. Even if some of those decisions aren't good, I still have time to course-correct. More importantly, all those good decisions have created momentum to drive scale and speed in my business before other leaders have even made one. I'm always moving forward by making up my mind fast.

I'm going to teach you how to make better decisions faster, to gain a major advantage.

When faced with a decision, effective leaders know how to choose a course of action expeditiously. They don't rush, but they also don't hem and haw for days. They are decisive, taking action on the information they have available to them. They know that inaction and indecision can result in disaster.

Facebook founder Mark Zuckerberg wears the same outfit everyday because that's one less decision that he has to make: "I really want to clear my life to make it so that I have to make as few decisions as possible about anything except how to best serve this community," Zuckerberg said, after clarifying that he had "multiple same shirts." Successful people understand that you need to streamline the decision-making process.

In many cases, the response—yes or no, go or no-go—matters less than taking action without wasting time. You don't want to spend so much time thinking about it that you lose sight of the bigger picture.

## The Downside of Avoiding Decisions

Take Ford Motor company and its former CEO Mark Fields. Fields took the helm in 2014, replacing Alan Mulally, who is credited with guiding Ford through the Great Recession. But where Mulally's challenge had been keeping the ship afloat, Fields's task was to lead the company from the old era to the new while maintaining profitability.

That new era included competitors that Ford probably never imagined would be in the car business—Tesla, Uber, and Alphabet— and issues the company's CEO had never had to face.

Unfortunately, under Fields, priorities became clouded and decision-making slowed. Forbes contributor Bryce Hoffman, author of *American Icon: Alan Mulally and the Fight to Save Ford Motor Company*, reported that Ford's leadership team was becoming increasingly frustrated with Fields' "gradual loss of focus and a growing concern the company was moving away from the clear and compelling vision and relentless implementation process that was Mulally's legacy."

Instead of staying the course that Mulally had laid out, Fields began dismantling the strategy and vision of his predecessor. Unfortunately, the vision and strategy he replaced it with was less clear and much less effective. One insider told Hoffman that at Ford, "Our priorities became clouded, and that really slowed decision making."

While established competitors General Motors, Toyota, and Volkswagen began "making bold, visible moves to prepare for an electrified, self-driving, shared-mobility future," reported The Motley Fool, Ford's sense of urgency was lacking or non-existent.

Ford's board of directors had fewer problems moving quickly to replace Fields, after recognizing that expedited decision-making was needed. The shakeup was in part because, according to Bill Ford, "Bureaucracy and hierarchy overwhelmed what could be faster decision making," Ford said. "The clock speed at which the world is moving, and our competitors, really requires us to make decisions at a faster pace… And we have to trust our people to move fast. It's not command and control."

To reinforce that need for speed, in his first 100 days, the new CEO, Jim Hackett, started enforcing a "shot clock" on lingering decisions, to try and reverse the slow speed with which choices had previously been made.

### A Steady Stream of Choices

According to a widely-cited statistic, American adults make as many as 35,000 decisions a day. That includes the mundane "Should I bring an umbrella?" to higher impact matters that might include, "Is this candidate the best choice for this position, or should we keep looking?"

 *American adults make as many as 35,000 decisions a day.*

Making a decision makes progress possible; indecision and procrastination can be stagnating and costly. No decision means no action, no progress, no movement forward. Putting aside the decision about a new hire might mean losing the best candidate to another firm in the meantime.

Of course, it's easy to overthink things and make simple choices more complex than they need to be. The key is breaking down each choice into the simplest of questions. If you have a framework in place for weighing your options, you should be able to move quickly.

## How to Decide

Out of the 35,000 decisions you make in a day, 98 percent should be made instantly. For example, should I wear a black shirt or red, should I brush my teeth or not (yes, you should), and do I want cream in my coffee are all simple, split-second decisions. Just as decisions like whether you should buy a $100 pair of tennis shoes should also be instant; don't waste time deliberating over such small purchases.

Only 2 percent of your daily decisions should not be made instantly. You should make them quickly, but you may need to spend some time weighing your options. For harder decisions, consider:

- Whether you will be put in any physical danger
- Whether the cost of the decision is more than $1,000

For example, should you bungee jump or skydive, or should you hire a new employee that will add $5,000 to your monthly payroll or sign a six-year multimillion dollar office space lease? These types of decisions fall into the two percent but still need to be made quickly. Below I've created the two percent decision-making process.

### The 2 Percent Decision-Making Process

To start, break down your decision to improve the quality and quantity of decisions you make. Here are some guidelines to follow:

**What do you really want?** When faced with a decision, no matter how trivial or how critical, start by getting clear about your ultimate goal.

Do you really want to hire more employees to grow your company, or is your true goal higher revenue? If higher sales is your goal, not empire-building, you may not need to add head count. Or if you're trying to decide about whether to change the company dress code, take a step back to consider what's driving that decision? What do you think a dress code change will do?

Make sure your decision will support, not hinder, your business goals.

**Gather supporting data.** What is it you need to know to make an informed decision? Odds are good you already know enough, or close to it. You probably have an inkling of what to do next, but if you feel you don't, quickly pull together key pieces of information to help you make your decision.

In evaluating products, you might investigate must-have features. In considering services, you might weigh the vendors' track record or proximity to your office.

"Don't make a project out of it," as copywriter Bob Bly has been known to say when cautioning against making a mountain out of a molehill. Decide what you need to know and then find it, delegating as needed to team members for speed.

**Lay out pros and cons.** Sometimes it helps to visually break down the advantages and disadvantages of each choice, especially when you have more than two.

Create two columns, one for the pros and one for the cons associated with each choice. This exercise isn't about automatically choosing the one that has the most pros and the fewest cons—it's about helping you become more objective about your decision. Make a list and compare the upsides and downsides of each choice:

| Pros | Cons |
|------|------|
|      |      |
|      |      |
|      |      |
|      |      |
|      |      |
|      |      |

**Go with your gut.** Most decisions come down to gut feel. Fortunately, your gut is pretty accurate. It represents all that you currently know about the topic. So what is your gut telling you?

In situations where multiple people are impacted, you may want to consider two more steps in your decision-making process:

**Align key stakeholders.** Even when you're the CEO or founder, it's smart to involve others when your decision is likely to cause some employees, customers, vendors, or community partners discomfort. Getting buy-in can boost understanding and enthusiasm and help others start thinking ahead to what comes next.

In cases of widespread organizational change, having a posse or entourage alongside you who support your decision ups your odds of success.

**Communicate.** The worst thing you can do is fail to share information about your decision in a timely manner. Good or bad, your employees want to know what's going on. So as soon as you know what your next move is, tell them.

Then tell them what it means for them. You're merging with a competitor? Will there be cuts? How about promotion opportunities? Will anyone have to relocate? Will you be adding staff? Share what you know and tell them when you'll know more.

**Set the timer for nine minutes.** Many experts advocate putting a time-limit on the decision-making process and I agree. Some decisions you should be able to make in seconds—which route to take to work, whether to renew your annual Lifelock protection or not, or donating to your alma mater are all fairly easy calls. Don't spend more than 10 seconds on these.

And then there are the decisions that require some weighing of factors, like cost, opportunity, risk, and time. You may need to gather some more input to understand the pros and cons of some decisions, or to reach out to team members for their perspectives. But once you have all that, nine minutes is enough time to make an informed choice. You have a good idea of what to do right now, so go with it. Move on from your current decision to something else. The more decisions you make, the bigger your potential for success.

But don't think that you need more time. In fact, research has found that making decisions under duress can actually yield better results. Malcolm Gladwell refers to the concept of "rapid cognition" in his book *Blink*, which is, essentially, using your knowledge, experience, and skill to filter out extraneous information and focus on what really matters when making a decision. It's accurate guessing based on what you already know. During high stress situations, the part of the brain responsible for rapid cognition steps up to guide you.

I remember being presented with a major business opportunity. We had the chance to bid on work with one of our clients' major competitors. If we pursued it we could lose our current client, which was worth about $1 million in revenue. But if we won the competitor's business, we stood to make $2 million - plus it was a bigger name brand.

My team was so excited about the opportunity. I also got caught up in their enthusiasm. We could win $2 million in business but also stood to lose $1 million. This was a big decision and I needed to decide quickly. So I used my process:

What I wanted: I wanted not to lose what I had but replace it with a bigger account. I knew I couldn't keep both due to competitive issues.

I gathered supporting data: I explored what it would be like working with this new client, how they treated their vendors, how long they typically partnered with vendors, whether they paid their bills on time, and more. Through some quick phone calls and a little online research, I learned that they typically re-bid their business every year and were always 90 or more days past due in paying their vendors.

I broke down the pros and cons of pursuing this new account:

| Pros | Cons |
|---|---|
| Potentially more money | Bad reputation |
| | Re-bid every year |
| | Slow pay |
| | Could lose current client and not win new, ending up with $0 |

Went with my gut: I passed on pursuing this account.

Aligned my team and communicated to the broader organization: I knew my team would be disappointed so I quickly expressed the reason this account wasn't a good fit for us, sharing the pros and cons with them. Instead we worked on a plan to grow our existing account.

We actually told our client that we had passed up the opportunity with their competition and was soon able to grow that account to more than $2 million, thereby achieving our goal of increasing revenue without losing our existing account.

## The Trickle-Down Effect

While you might not think delayed decision-making is a big deal, the fact is, others could quite possibly be stalled until you decide. If you haven't approved an employee's travel budget for that conference in a few months, she can't register and take advantage of the early bird discount—which costs you money. If you haven't conducted personnel reviews for the year, employees haven't received important feedback or increases, which might lead your superstar performer to start interviewing elsewhere. If you haven't decided which ad agency is getting your business for an upcoming campaign, no one can begin brainstorming creative approaches. If you haven't updated your website in months, you are most certainly missing out on potential new business. And if you haven't called your attorney about that cease-and-desist letter you received regarding your company name, you could soon be shut down. Inaction is deadly.

As hours stretch into days and even weeks, your team's momentum can slow to a crawl. And since you set the pace as a leader, your glacial decision-making speed becomes the standard for everyone working with you.

By moving slowly, you're telling people that you value examining every option from all possible directions more than you prize quick decision-making and forward movement.

If that's not how you want to be perceived, *make a decision*. Make it quickly and encourage those around you to do the same. It's okay if they make the wrong decision every once in a while because the number of good ones will probably far outweigh the bad.

You are their role model. If you want them to be decisive, *you* have to be decisive.

### Decisions Are Often Reversible

In many cases, fear of making a mistake causes people to freeze. They put off deciding on something so they don't get it wrong—justifying the inaction by saying they're gathering more information. Have you ever put the brakes on to avoid making the wrong choice? When you do that, you risk nixing any chance of making progress and grabbing new opportunities because you're stuck.

Decisions make progress possible.

Fact is, few decisions are immutable. You can often change your mind once you learn more, or you can make a few more decisions to optimize your first one.

Say you decide to move into a larger office space and a week after signing the lease, you land a major contract that will require so many more employees that the new space will be too small. Or maybe that's your fear—that you'll be locked into space that you will quickly outgrow.

The solution if that happens? Talk to your new landlord about other properties you could move to, how you can expand the space you just leased, other space you can take over in the building, or options allowed by your "out" clause. Depending on the size of that new contract, you may decide to pay to get out of it and move elsewhere.

Maybe you decide it's time to join a gym to get in shape on your lunch hour. If the next day a friend talks you into joining a different health club so you can work out together, you might be able to cancel your membership. Some states even let you back out of a contract like that if you act within three days after signing. If not, you might be able to sell your membership to someone else.

The point is, there are plenty of workarounds once you make a decision that you realize wasn't the best. But at least in making it, you made it possible to move forward. And your team will thank you for that.

## Speed Read

- People are faced with 35,000+ decisions a day. If you're not making decisions fast, you will lose. Ninety-eight percent of those decisions should be made instantly.

- The 2 Percent Decision-Making Process helps you work through those decisions that can't be made instantly: 1) What do you really want? 2) Gather supporting data 3) Lay out pros and cons 4) Go with your gut 5) Align key stakeholders 6) Communicate 7) Set the timer for 9 minutes.

- In most cases, it doesn't matter what you decide as long as you decide something fast. Many decisions are reversible.

# Create Urgency

To survive in today's fast-paced, global economy, you must create a culture of urgency. Everyone, from your employees and vendors to your clients, must act quickly, understanding that their success depends on it. It's not optional, it's essential.

Businesses that operate with a sense of urgency grow and those that don't, die. If you aren't acting with a sense of urgency, your customers will go elsewhere. Customers today expect things fast, whether it's a call back, delivery of their order, or an email response. Since they expect and demand a fast response, it's up to you to shift your priorities to make it happen.

If you can't keep up, it's over. If you don't create that urgency internally, you'll never gain traction and you'll never scale. Your competitors will crush you. You need to be urgent in everything you do, from conducting meetings, to delivering proposals, the more volume the better the outcome. Your need to condition your organization to work with urgency.

I truly believe that if you're not creating urgency, you may be creating complacency. Good enough will be good enough, yes, but it won't be good enough for massive success. It won't be good enough to get ahead and gain a competitive advantage. If you really want something, you need to have a burning desire to take action now—on everything in your business.

Urgency is a commitment to getting results, now. It's a preference for taking action immediately, repeatedly.

And as the owner of your business, you set the pace for how quickly tasks get done in your company. If you create an atmosphere or culture where things "have to get done asap," those around you will strive to get things done asap. This is important as the pace of change has increased exponentially in the last couple of decades thanks to our increasing reliance on technology.

According to Harvard Business School professor John Kotter, author of *A Sense of Urgency*:

"…the world is moving faster and faster—there's no way in the world, unless you've got this sense of urgency, that you can move and maneuver in a smart way to win."

In every business I've ever owned, whether we're talking about serving clients, launching campaigns, or even just scheduling meetings, I tried to foster a sense of urgency. I did that by making it clear what we, as a company, needed to focus on. Everyone had their individual roles to play and I had expectations for what they needed to accomplish, expressed as performance goals, which made it possible for us to progress at warp speed. When you have clarity, priorities, and incentives all aligned, as a business you can move fast.

## Speed with Purpose

If you can instill a sense of urgency into your team, everyone will work faster, priorities will help them work smarter, and by having goals that are in sync, greater results will be achieved sooner.

However, taking action simply for the sake of completing a task isn't enough. As Kotter says, having urgency means "not to just have a meeting today, it's to have a meeting *that accomplishes something* today." The whole point of urgency is obtaining results in less time. If the task you're working on has little chance of generating progress toward your desired goal, there's no point in spending time on it. Each initiative or action needs to have a purpose—a reason for doing it.

Activity does not necessarily signal a sense of urgency, nor does it guarantee that meaningful results will be achieved. In many companies, activity is just activity—often useless.

Everyone also needs to understand that they have a role to play in achieving the desired results. The only way to make headway is when everyone in the company understands they need to participate—when employees see their own role as inconsequential to the larger objective, the more complacent they become, explains Kotter.

## Get Clear About Your Goals

A few years ago, the CEO of Klipfolio, Allan Wille, and his team set a goal of tripling the company's recurring revenue by the end of the year. Without adding additional resources, that was a stretch goal and he knew they would need to create a sense of urgency to achieve that objective within 12 months. So the company created a tool to spark "a feeling that work has to be done NOW." Explains Wille:

> "We issued our employees what looked like bingo cards. But instead of there being numbers in the squares on the cards, each square contained a target to be met. There were targets for leads,

targets for sales, targets for features to be developed—targets for each department to meet within a specific time frame."

It worked. Thanks to specific goals, each employee knew what he or she needed to do to support the company's bigger goal. "The result was a burst of creativity and activity across the whole company," says Wille.

Granted, the sense of urgency was man-made—it was artificial and designed solely to support Klipfolio's internal growth targets. And that's okay. Helping employees understand specifically how they can support their employer's larger goals, whether they include sales growth, geographic expansion, new product roll-outs, reduced safety incidents, or some other metric, makes it possible for them to contribute. Adding a sense of urgency can push workers to place a higher priority on such tasks, to ensure they get done sooner rather than later.

 *Urgency is a commitment to getting results, now.*

## Six Ways to Create a Sense of Urgency

Wanting everyone to buy in to the importance of urgency at work is much easier said than done. To persuade everyone to shift their thinking and approach, you'll want to try these tactics:

**Focus on outcomes**. It's very easy for all of us to fill our days with activities that have no noticeable impact on our short-term or long-term goals. We can waste a lot of time on tasks and must-dos that really shouldn't be done at all if we were hyper-focused on a particular objective. To help employees make this shift from completing tasks to achieving objectives, remind them regularly of what they're working toward. Ask them how what they're currently doing is making progress toward their desired outcome. Regularly reorienting them toward the outcome you want them to be focused on can help retrain them to invest their time and energy on high impact activities.

**Make decisions fast.** One of the best ways to impress upon employees the need for a sense of urgency is if you yourself act quickly. Make up your mind fast, or delegate to someone else immediately. Demonstrate that making a decision quickly, even without perfect information, is better than no decision at all. Don't leave decisions or employees hanging when it comes to answers. Decide and move on. Next!

**Establish consequences for slow performance.** In addition to modeling a sense of urgency, you may also want to communicate the downsides of failing to act quickly. Some employees are motivated by a carrot (incentive) and some need the threat of a negative action (stick) to fall in line. Explain what can happen if everyone does their part to help reach your goal, which might be sales growth, number of new clients, progress on developing a product prototype—whatever it is, spell out what you're working toward. And then warn what may happen if that goal is not reached. Perhaps slow performers will be shown the door or be placed on a different career track. You decide what's appropriate.

**Discourage time wasting.** Along the same lines as rooting out workers who lack a sense of urgency, help employees recognize activities that may not contribute to reaching your goal. Question whether every person invited really needs to attend certain meetings or suggest that meeting lengths be cut in half, for example. Identify tasks or projects that are taking up more time than they need to, or that involve more people than they should.

**Remove obstacles.** One thing guaranteed to slow your progress and quash that sense of urgency is a roadblock that gets in the way of completing a critical task. To keep everyone moving forward quickly, anticipate what obstacles or bottlenecks may appear and proactively eliminate them. Whether it's a policy, such as expenses over $100 have to be approved by three people, for example, or a technology issue, such as low bandwidth, or a situation that must first be addressed, take care of it and communicate that to your team. That helps underscore the importance of working quickly.

**Recognize role models**. Praise and reward employees who get it, those who routinely exhibit a sense of urgency and who energize others as a result. In addition to specific rewards for hitting defined target goals, publicly giving employees a pat on the back can be just as meaningful to those on the receiving end. Let them know you appreciate their attitude and approach to getting things done quickly.

## Moving Quickly Past Mistakes

If you're wondering how to ramp up the pace of work without also seeing an increase in mistakes, you can't. Mistakes are going to happen, and probably more frequently since you're no longer aiming for perfection with every task. That's okay.

Mistakes are actually good. Mistakes mean you're making progress. So move quickly, get out front, and don't sweat the small errors that are inevitable. In no time you'll be so far ahead of your competition that your mistakes really won't matter.

Being first is much more important than being perfect. The market is moving so fast that if you don't get out ahead of the competition, you'll lose out on opportunities.

As a digital marketing agency, my firm was constantly reinventing itself to remain market leader. You can't stand still and expect to stay out front. That meant that every six months or so, I would redesign our website to reflect our thinking about what was working in online marketing. We often incorporated a new feature or tool we wanted to showcase.

The first few times I told our team we needed to revamp the website and asked how long it would take, they would tell me two to three months.

"We have to have this in three weeks," I would tell them. I knew it wouldn't be perfect if they were working at that pace, but it was more important to me for us to get it out there than to have it be completely error-free.

They got it done in three weeks.

For a couple of years this became our dance. I would ask how long it was going to take to makeover the website and my team would tell me two to three months. I would insist we needed it in three weeks. And we got it done in three weeks.

Eventually, everyone adjusted to the new pace. They knew it had to be done in three weeks and it always was. And because we were able to turn things around so quickly, we were always the first to roll out new design approaches or online marketing solutions. That attracted new accounts, and then larger accounts. Our reputation quickly grew as an innovative, fast-paced agency. And we were.

We scaled quickly because we were regularly attracting more business from organizations that wanted to work at the same speed as we were.

Urgency enables speed. Speed attracts business. Business enables scaling. Don't take your foot off the gas.

## Speed Read

- Urgency is a commitment to getting results by taking action now, not later.
- Six ways to create a sense of urgency include: 1) Focus on outcomes 2) Make decisions fast 3) Establish consequences for slow performance 4) Discourage time wasting 5) Remove obstacles 6) Recognize role models.
- Don't let a fear of mistakes or failure slow your progress— mistakes will be made but if you move ahead full-speed, you'll get past any errors that much faster.

# The One-Page Attack
# and Conquer Plan

'm sure you've heard about the importance of a plan for your business. And right now you're probably picturing one of those long documents companies prepare to aid in explaining their business concept to outsiders. Business plans are typically used to pursue startup or growth financing or to study the impact of various courses of action. They're also fairly detailed, with five years of financial projections, plenty of charts and graphs, and a lot of bullshit—because, really, who knows what the market is going to look like in five years?!

I've used this document to take companies from hundreds of thousands of dollars to hundreds of millions. It's your game plan. It's everything that needs to be done.

Coaches use one-page game plans to manage each competition, they don't bring their huge playbook. *You* don't need a playbook.

And that's not what I'm talking about here.

You don't need a full-blown business plan unless you're looking for investors or lenders. What you *do* need is a simple internal strategic plan to ensure you're operating at peak speed and efficiency. Without it, you're toast.

The type of plan I want you to create is what I call a one-page attack and conquer plan. Its goal is setting priorities for your company that everyone can follow and get behind. It's simple, it's clear, and it's shared with everyone who works for you. After all, if your employees don't understand what your priorities are for the year, how are they going to effectively pitch in to help? They can't.

Sharing your one-page plan with everyone will create alignment and clarity about your company's priorities and goals for the year.

Every successful company I've run and owned has created and used a one-page plan. Without one, we would have failed, and you will too unless you get clear and convey your goals concisely.

## The Five Sections of a One-Page Attack and Conquer Plan

Your one-page plan should be broken down into five different sections that, together, form a road map for how you're going to achieve your goals in record time. Of course, it's easier to move quickly when everyone is working in sync toward your objectives.

1.  **Goals and actions**. You need no more than four to six annual goals, including an overarching revenue goal, a profit goal, and other ancillary types of goals. Then you have to build global quarterly action plans against those goals that translate into monthly, weekly, and daily action items and plans with clear owners and accountability.

The most important thing is committing to four to six goals and from there creating the key deliverables to start working toward that goal. Then you assign an owner, who assigns the task to the team to complete. You need to set accountability. That's the secret sauce – delegating and following up to make sure it gets done.

Once you put a goal on paper it means nothing until you assign it to people and follow up and measure results. You can say your goal is to hit $10 million in revenue, but until you break down what that looks like in terms of quarterly, monthly, weekly, and daily revenue, and assign action items to people who will complete them, you're never going to get there.

2. **Core values**. What are your four core values? What characteristics or skills will make or break your company? These core values are what you're looking for in new employees and what you'll evaluate future decisions against.

At one of my companies, our core values were: creative, fearless, curious, and strategic. We knew that if we had those skills and mindsets on our team, we would win.

So I decided to really drive home those core values by buying life-size statues of characters who embodied those traits; I placed the statues around our offices. I had Spiderman for creative, a 12-foot Hulk for fearless, Yoda for curious, and a six-foot Army guy for strategic. You can bet the office was constantly reminded of what the company valued every time they walked by the Hulk or Yoda.

3. **Who/What/Why**. This section of your plan makes it clear who you are, what your company does, and why people want to buy it.

The benefit of simplifying even the most basic concepts is that you increase the odds that everyone understands what you're working toward and what you offer your clients. Once these are clear for everyone on your team, you cut down on meaningless conversations with prospects— they're either in your target market and interested in what you sell or they're not. And if they're not, move on.

4. **Priorities**. Set no more than six to eight priorities. Otherwise, you'll spread everyone too thin and your true focus will dissipate and become unclear. You'll be more profitable the fewer your priorities.

Companies that struggle typically are trying to do too much all at once. Maybe they're trying to rein in spending while also expanding their geographic footprint, hiring new members of their management team, and rolling out an innovative new product line. While this is a made-up example, it's not unusual. It's also ridiculous.

No successful company could achieve more than one, or perhaps two, of these priorities simultaneously. And some are even mutually exclusive—you can't cut expenses and expand at the same time.

A better approach is to choose a handful of high impact priorities that everyone on your team is confident will have a material impact on your bottom line. Go with those and only those.

5. **Revenue focus**. To grow quickly, you need to be clear about where your revenue is going to come from. What are your distribution channels, profit centers, and revenue targets?

That is, where is your revenue going to originate and what are your sales targets? You need a system to measure your financial performance and be able to identify where the sale originated. Was it your marketing team's new social media campaign? Did a member of your corporate sales team follow up persistently until the client signed on the dotted line?

Introduce systems that will help you track a sales prospect through your sales process.

And be clear about who your ideal client is and then invest your resources in finding and selling them. Don't waste time closing clients you don't want.

Make sure your whole team understands who your best customers are and where they're located so that they have an easier time of connecting with them and successfully selling them.

| CORE VALUES | Curious – We always ask what happened, why and what we can do to make it better<br>Fearless – We are not afraid to try something new and take on any challenge<br>**Strategic** – We stay focused on the big picture and always think two steps ahead<br>**Creative** – The best way to deal with problems is to think of an answer no one thought possible |
| --- | --- |

| | |
|---|---|
| **WHO<br>WHAT<br>WHY** | **Who you are** – The performance marketing & conversion optimization agency for X<br>**What you do** – We use digital marketing to generate qualified leads and sales for our clients<br>**What proof do you have** – We improve on average our clients result s by 40%<br>**Why you do it** – We believe that digital marketing is the future and most effective way to market<br>**Why people want it** – We are the thought leaders in our space and are so confident in our results that we will work based on pay-per-performance. We don't WIN unless our clients WIN. |
| **PRIORITIES** | Increase marketing awareness, increase qualified lead generation, increased sales closing %, streamlined operations and increase margin %. |
| **REVENUE FOCUS** | Flawlessly execute marketing, sales, PR and account retention/growth plans<br>Measure and optimize everything on the one-page attack and conqueror plan<br><br>Target Market: (Listed in priority)<br>• Retail (Brick & Mortar / eCommerce)<br>• CPG<br>• Franchise<br><br>Parameters to follow:<br>• 100 M + revenue<br>• Located in Dallas, Houston, Portland<br>• Spend 5 M + on digital media and agency fee |

| Goals & Actions | |
|---|---|
| **Goals for 2014 – Achieved by 12/20/14** | **Actions – to be achieved by or before 3/20/14 (Q1)** |
| 1. Generate XM in fee in new business<br>   • 1 total $xM+ clients<br>   • 2 total $xM+ clients<br>   • 1 total $xK + clients<br>   • 2 total $xK + projects<br>2. 30% Profit<br>3. 14 National PR pieces<br>4. Implement account management and CRM software<br>5. No account loss and 10%+ in organic growth | 1. Finalize and implement marketing, sales, PR and account retention/growth plans<br>2. Completed 4 PR<br>3. Implement sales force and Blue software<br>4. Completed all client QBR's and presented all clients with additional ways to grow their business<br>5. Clearly communicate to the entire company the one page plan and then implement micro-plans that latter up to the One-page. Incentives everyone and hold everyone accountable. |

*Here's a sample one-page attack plan I used in one of my businesses. To get your own blank one-page attack plan, visit JudgeGraham.com.*

## Measuring Success

While many companies actually create plans, so few ever measure results or hold people accountable for what they said they would accomplish. Quantifying your goals is critical, otherwise you'll never be successful.

It's much harder to argue with dollar figures or output counts, so make sure to convert every goal or milestone to a quantitative value. Customer satisfaction can be measured through follow-up surveys. And public relations success can be measured through the number of press releases distributed or the equivalent ad value of coverage earned. The only way you can measure success is if you have numbers to work with.

Start with annual goals and then break them down into quarterly milestones and daily progress, which you should be measuring. Set 90-day targets and check in with everyone daily to see what steps they've taken to get closer to that quarterly (90-day) objective.

Make sure to incentivize everyone, offering bonuses, trips, days off, or other perks to reinforce that everyone will benefit if you collectively hit your goals. You can even set up performance tiers that make it clear who gets how much based on individual and company results.

Assign team leaders who will work with their teams to create microplans designed to systematically progress toward achievement of your goals. And then measure performance regularly to confirm everyone understands their job.

*You don't need a full-blown business plan unless you're looking for investors or lenders.*

### Create a Theme

In addition to laying out the specific tasks and initiatives for the coming year, you'll also want to create a theme or rally cry that conveys your plan instantly. A theme is kind of like a slogan for the year.

During March Madness, you often see the players with special shirts printed just for the event with their team's theme on it—their theme for the season. The University of Michigan's, for example, was "Do More Say Less." Butler University's was "Gritty not Pretty." And the University of Houston's was "For the City."

These themes represented what the team was collectively focusing on during the 2018 basketball season. Those words were a way of unifying the players' collective focus in their pursuit of a championship win.

You need to do the same for your team of workers—create a theme that reflects what you're all working toward this year.

One year the theme for my company was "Be Bullish and Win." I wanted everyone to be optimistic—hence the bull market reference— and confident that we could achieve our collective goals. I wanted everyone to charge forward.

In addition to coming up with a theme slogan, I used that phrase in a number of ways. I created t-shirts emblazoned with the words "Be Bullish and Win," posted the words around our offices, and signed my emails with that theme, so that my employees were constantly reminded of what we were aiming to do.

## Launch Your Plan

Once you've come up with a theme that reflects your focus for the year, don't just pass it out as a memo—get everyone together! Hold an all-hands meeting to bring everyone together in one place to be introduced to the plan for the year.

It should be part presentation, part pep rally. You want your employees to leave that meeting pumped up and enthused! They should be excited about where the company is headed, the role they can play, and the potential rewards they can earn by contributing.

I know that this can work because I've witnessed the difference developing a one-page plan can have on an organization.

At one of my companies, I distinctly recall sitting around a conference table with my leadership team one December wondering, "How are we going to scale?" We were barely growing when the market opportunities were obvious. We knew we had to make some changes or we'd be out of business within the year.

So we introduced a planning process and a structure for evaluating our progress. Our one-page plan that came out of that meeting had clarity, alignment, energy, and accountability. Immediately after that meeting, each leader met with their individual teams and set team goals and performance expectations. Then we met regularly to measure our progress toward our larger goals.

Within 12 months we had achieved growth that exceeded 35 percent when the prior year our growth was flat at around 4.5 percent. The turnaround was remarkable.

We stayed on that trajectory thanks to our new planning process— the process that allowed us to scale with speed.

## Speed Read

- Your one-page attack and conquer plan is a simple, single sheet of paper with 5 sections: 1) goals and actions, 2) core values, 3) who/what/why you sell what you sell, 4) your priorities, and 5) revenue focus.

- Once you have your one-page plan, you have to create a theme that is a constant reminder of what your whole team is working toward. If they're not onboard, you'll fail. Create a slogan or phrase that you repeat that reflects what you're trying to achieve. Post it on walls and have it printed on swag that you give out to employees and customers as a way of showing your commitment to the concept.

- Measuring your progress and performance is the only way to ensure you hit your goals. You must quantify them. Trying to measure such vague concepts as customer loyalty or productivity doesn't work unless you can tie it to a quantifiable measure, such as number of purchases in a year or calls taken in an hour.

# Make All Systems, Processes, and Delivery Simple

One of the biggest keys to managing a well-oiled speed machine is to have tight and simple processes. If you're not running your business efficiently, you can't scale.

You need to have established policies and procedures. By defining processes for internal tasks, you can streamline decisions and activities. This is true for everything from hiring to firing to purchasing to pursuing partnerships with other businesses; processes can reduce inefficiencies. You save time, money, and can improve the quality of products and services you sell clients.

By establishing approved processes for completing certain tasks, employees can stay focused on producing what they've been hired to produce, whether they're software developers, automotive mechanics, executive chefs, or anything in between. Reducing the amount of administrative decision-making employees need to do allows them to stay focused on where they can make the greatest contribution to revenue generation. After all, that's why you hired them, right?

However, there is also a point at which processes and systems can get in the way of revenue generation. If a big portion of anyone's time is spent developing systems and processes, rather than generating revenue, you're slowing down progress. You can't scale, much less scale with speed, if you're getting caught in the weeds.

Take a step back and ask how much time will be saved by introducing a process or system to address a particular situation. Is this a one-time event or a scenario that occurs weekly? For example, are you dealing with the process for finding a new location, which likely only needs to occur every few years, or a system for handling expense reimbursement, which is probably something you have to handle daily or weekly?

### Don't Go Overboard

Back in the 1990s, many major corporations were hot to win the Malcolm Baldrige National Quality Award. It quickly became the most coveted recognition among the Fortune 500 as a sign of quality products and processes.

While the award itself was designed to recognize organizations that had achieved performance excellence—breaking down processes throughout the company, documenting them, measuring them, and taking steps to achieve incremental improvement across the board—contenders for the award quickly got bogged down in process documentation. Departments were soon required to document every step in every process under their control. This probably added a lot of value for manufacturing teams, but I have a hard time picturing much value from having assistants document how to take a phone memo or purchasing reps documenting how to fill out a purchase order.

In a *Harvard Business Review* article, Xerox, the 1989 winner, admitted it spent $800,000 on consultants to help guide the company through the Baldrige application process, and Corning, a finalist the same year, reportedly invested 14,000 man hours in preparation.

That's a lot of time and money spent documenting processes that may not really have needed to be documented in the first place, other than for an honor that is likely to have little to no impact on revenue.

Yes, processes and systems are critical for scaling with speed, as long as you don't become so obsessed with establishing systems that you lose sight of the real goal—massive revenue creation.

## Eliminating Unneeded Processes

To keep everyone focused on revenue generation, you need to simplify every aspect of your business. Activities that take employees away from revenue-generating activities include:

- Processes that slow down or prevent the customer from buying from you
- Expense reports
- Time tracking
- Internal bloated processes (you never need more than three people to approve anything)
- Time off
- CRM systems that are too complicated

If you want to keep things simple and have speed and momentum, you need to ensure those processes you have in place make you feel confident about the decisions being made by others and empower your people to make smart decisions independently. Your internal systems need to be simple and easy, but effective, to allow everyone in the organization to make decisions. When that happens, you have speed and scale.

I learned this first hand at the digital marketing agency by doing it wrong and implementing too many processes and systems. We were growing so quickly that I was implementing new tracking tools left and right to be certain we weren't missing any opportunities for improvement and growth.

One of the pieces of data we began tracking was time—how each of our 200 employees was spending his or her time at work. I thought that if we monitored where that time was being spent, we could each do a better job of improving productivity. Also, our clients wanted reports on who was doing what on their behalf.

However, everyone hated tracking time. They hated it so much that they generally waited until the very last minute to try and put a report together, looking back over the last week to see where they had been, what had been due, and guessing at how much time they spent here and there. The time reports were totally inaccurate and, on top of that, my employees were pissed about having to take the time to report on their every move. We had bad data coming in, so we really couldn't do anything worthwhile or useful with the results we were seeing—after all, they were totally made up.

Once I realized how little value we were getting from time tracking, I told everyone to stop. There was no point. And I told our clients, "We don't track time, we provide value."

While I'll admit I was initially nervous about backing off of the time-tracking—it's how agencies do business, after all—the results spoke for themselves. By getting rid of this time-consuming activity, we saw an improvement in client results (probably because people could get back to being creative) and a 3 to 5 percent increase in revenue, which was a large percentage given that we were experiencing 35 percent total growth.

After witnessing the profound effect removing a process had on our company, I went ahead and eliminated 50 percent of the processes I had introduced. Yes, the goal had been to standardize some administrative processes, but the ultimate goal was efficiency and profitability. Using those yardsticks, I cut out any process that wasn't having a positive impact on our bottom line.

The result was that employees felt more empowered to make decisions. They didn't need to consult a manual or follow some scripted system—they could decide for themselves, on the spot, what the best solution was.

Turns out, keeping the decision-making process as simple as possible is actually more important than adding burdensome steps and policies no one wants to follow. When you understand what it takes to deliver value, you can strip away all the "administrivia" that's doing no one any good. That included daily time tracking.

> *By defining processes for completing internal tasks, you can streamline decisions and activities.*

## Don't Be Afraid to Bail

One area where we weren't afraid to invest was in software systems to manage ourselves and our clients. In fact, we spent hundreds of thousands of dollars on a new project management system to help us get more done in less time. It was the best software on the market and we spent months integrating it into our existing system in the interests of helping us scale with speed.

It took us four months to realize the new system wasn't working. It wasn't doing all that we had hoped it would and, in fact, was impeding our progress.

Most companies would continue to use it as a way to justify the huge expenditure. Not us. Once we saw that it was slowing down our operation and causing us to focus more on processes than on client work, we ditched it. Why continue to use a system—no matter what the cost—if it's costing you money in lost time and productivity every day.

Simplify your operations by introducing systems that support your work and get rid of any that get in the way, even if you've spent a lot of money on it. What's that saying—don't throw good money after bad.

### Streamline, Streamline, Streamline

Do all you can to simplify how you do business and how you serve your customers. People hate unnecessary steps in business processes. If it takes pressing five different options in your phone system to get to the person they need, that's about four too many. The same is true about everything else in your business.

Look for ways to reduce steps people have to take to do what they want to do. That means taking steps to:

- **Accept all forms of payment.** Why limit yourself to a couple of platforms when it's easier and more convenient to allow customers to pay using the company they prefer, whether it's PayPal, Square, Stripe, cryptocurrency, or something else. Set it up once and never have to apologize that you "don't take that form of payment."

- **Make contract signatures a two-click process.** When you send out an agreement for signatures, don't make it a 20-minute ordeal to review and sign the agreement. Use a system like Docusign to allow customers to open a form and easily add their signature. Don't use 40-page contracts that customers will need to pay their attorney to review; keep the language simple and commonsense.

- **Make getting hold of a knowledgeable person easy.** Use Live Chat 24/7 or respond to emails and phone calls instantly to give customers the information they need.
- **Simplify returns.** Be like Zappos and allow customers to return products they've bought from you with no pushback or hassle. If they aren't happy with it, let them return it and provide a shipping label by email to allow them to do it quickly and easily.

Any interaction with the customer needs to be simple and flawless. The customer experience needs to be simple, fast, and easy. Evaluate all interaction points you have with customers to be sure they're impressed with how easy you are to do business with.

Checks and balances are critical in government and in your business, but don't allow your company to get bogged down in bureaucracy. That goes against everything scaling with speed is about.

Follow one rule here to be sure processes and systems will benefit your business: The process must make it easier or better for the customer, or we don't do it.

## Speed Read

- Business systems and processes can be useful in establishing standards, but they can also slow down progress and add unnecessary tasks. Be sure any new processes you introduce are helping employees work faster and better on behalf of your customers.
- Simplify internal processes by eliminating: 1) Processes that slow down or prevent the customer from buying from you 2) Expense reports 3) Time tracking 4) Internal bloated processes (you never need more than 3 people to approve anything) 5) Time off 6) CRM systems that are too complicated.

- Be easy to do business with. Accept all forms of payment. Make contract signatures a two-click process. Make getting hold of a knowledgeable person easy. Simplify returns.

# Part 4
# Energize Your Culture

*"Real culture is a game-changer."*
**– Judge Graham**

If you don't have a culture that understands speed and urgency, you lose. You have to energize and create a motivated environment that learns how to constantly be running and operating with massive expectations. Without that you'll never be able to scale a monster company.

There's no room for complacency, everything is fast. What takes you a week to do, your competitors take four or five. That's the kind of environment it takes to win. That's when you know you have a speed-driven culture.

It takes most people six to nine months to write a good book. It took me three to finish the book you're currently reading. I pulled together a team of motivated professionals who had a sense of urgency like mine. We built a micro-culture to complete a bestselling book in three months.

Getting everyone rowing together in the same direction can make scaling with speed so much easier and faster.

So make sure everyone knows their role and how they are expected to perform. Set targets along with offering rewards for achievement of those targets. Make it clear that everyone will benefit when the company reaches its objectives.

Taking care of your team, by demonstrating how valuable they are to your company, will establish a bond that is likely to keep them in place, working hard for your success, long-term.

# Commit Fully and Burn the Ships

The phrase burning the ships comes from the military and refers to intentionally cutting off your own retreat to force you to choose a course of action. People fail in business because they never really commit. You need to do some things that force you to be all-in or you will never be as successful as you could be.

I've already told you that hanging back and second-guessing your decisions won't get you anywhere. You need to start now. Dive in headfirst and put all your energy and resources into making your business a success. If you want to scale, you can't have one leg in and one leg out—you'll make headway much faster if both legs are invested.

Commit—burn those ships! Put so much pressure on yourself to succeed that it's your only option. Once you've committed, really committed, you're all in with no way to turn back.

That means:

- Quitting your job
- Maxing out your credit cards and investing your savings to start your business
- Uprooting your family and selling your home
- Taking on a line of credit to buy a building for your company

I've done all these and more. Because that's what it takes to achieve the level of success most people only dream of.

## There is Freedom in Committing

People talk about wanting success, but until you go all-in and do things that force you to commit, you never really do it. It's just talk. If you want to do this, you have to commit and take action. You've always dreamed of owning a business but until you get a line of credit and buy it, you're just dreaming.

Deciding that you will do all that you need to in order to be successful is committing. Being wishy-washy or half in will get in the way of your success.

If you're still working on your business on the side, moonlighting, you're not fully committed. Your day job is a crutch that takes the pressure off of your business success; if you don't hit your sales targets or you lose a customer, it's okay, because you can live off of your full-time salary, you may tell yourself. You're actually making it harder to achieve success because you have no external pressure. If you succeed or fail, it won't really affect your lifestyle.

You haven't committed.

I get that you may be scared of failing, which is why you hold onto that day job you hate. But the reality is that you won't be able to achieve success and full financial freedom until you are totally dependent on your business to provide for you. When you're all-in, you will find ways to get things done at a pace you never imagined—because you have no alternative. If you aren't successful you could be homeless, carless, and struggling to put food on the table.

People accomplish amazing things when they have to in order to survive. So burn the ship that's holding you back, whether it's your day job, a contract that's causing you to lose sleep or lose money, or a toxic relationship that's in the way of your success and happiness.

## Take Massive Action

Once you've made success your only option, it's time to invest all of your time, effort, and money in accomplishing your goals.

Grant Cardone, author of *The 10X Rule: The Only Difference Between Success and Failure*, says that by taking massive action (which is The 10X Rule) "you will dissolve fears, increase your belief in yourself, eliminate procrastination, and provide you with an overwhelming sense of purpose."

Cardone is known for taking massive action to obtain big results quickly—it's what his book is about, after all. Cardone applied this approach in his own life when he decided to make the transition from auto sales expert to general business sales coach in 2010.

Following the commitment to become the dominant sales consultant for the Fortune 500, Cardone moved from Louisiana to Miami, Florida. He leased a big corporate office and filled it with staff members and then got to work attracting new business. He increased the amount of outbound content by a factor of 10 and upped the amount of time he was spending on the business to 80 hours a week and managed to quickly increase annual revenue generated by 10X.

By doing what others refuse to do, either because it's hard or time-consuming, you will separate yourself from the market. You will conquer while they're still flailing around trying to decide where to focus.

As Nike says, "Just do it."

 *People talk about wanting success, but until you go all-in and do things that force you to commit, you never really do it.*

## Persistence Does Pay Off

Part of committing and conquering has to do with sticking with a task. One of the best examples of persistence that I've heard of involves Steve Jobs' pursuit of John Sculley to become the next CEO of Apple. He committed and then conquered.

In 1982, Apple needed to replace its president and Jobs recognized he was not yet up to the task. He first approached Don Estridge at IBM about the role but was turned down.

So Apple decided to take a different tack and, instead of pursuing a corporate technology leader, decided to focus instead on acquiring a consumer marketer with "the corporate polish that would play well on Wall Street," explains Walter Isaacson in his biography of Jobs.

John Sculley, then-president of the Pepsi-Cola division of PepsiCo became Jobs' target. Sculley's Pepsi Challenge advertising campaign had been a promotional coup for the company and vaulted him to superstar status. Isaacson said he was "the hottest consumer marketing wizard of the moment," with some sources referring to him as a "wunderkind." And he was Jobs' pick to run Apple. Jobs was going to hire him.

At the time, no big brand marketer had gone to Silicon Valley from the East Coast. Further, it was unprecedented for someone to come to a high-profile Silicon Valley company without a technical background. Jobs's plan was unconventional, to say the least.

The first meeting between Jobs and Sculley took place at Apple's headquarters in California around Christmas in 1982, when Sculley was in town to visit his children. Isaacson reported that Sculley was interested in the position but "still reluctant to leave Pepsi."

Then in January they met in New York, dining together at the Four Seasons restaurant and talking until close to midnight. According to Isaacson, Jobs told Sculley, "This has been one of the most exciting evenings in my whole life" as Sculley walked him back to the Carlyle. "I can't tell you how much fun I've had."

Their next meeting was in February, when Jobs flew east for a visit and took a limo to Sculley's home. In March, Sculley stopped in at Apple's Cupertino, Calif. headquarters on his way back from a Pepsi bottlers' convention in Hawaii, when Jobs unveiled the Macintosh. He told Sculley, "I want you to be the first person outside of Apple to see it." On the screen was a graphic presentation featuring Pepsi cans and caps dancing around with the Apple logo, reports Isaacson. Jobs' team had been told that the presentation was needed because Pepsi might place a large order of Macintoshes, not that Sculley could become their new leader.

Sculley refused to travel to meet with Jobs, reported the Heidrick & Struggles recruiter who ultimately placed Sculley, so Jobs came back to New York in March 1983 and "was able to convert the courtship into a blind and blinding romance," according to Isaacson. As they walked through Central Park towards the Central Park West condo Jobs was planning to buy, Jobs said, "I really think you're the guy. I want you to come and work with me. I can learn so much from you."

They continued talking out on the penthouse's terrace where Sculley asked for $1 million in salary and a $1 million signing bonus. Jobs agreed and then Sculley demurred. "Steve's head dropped as he stared at his feet," Isaacson recounted. "After a weighty, uncomfortable pause, he issued a challenge that would haunt me for days," says Sculley. "'Do you want to spend the rest of your life selling sugared water, or do you want a chance to change the world?'"

That line was what did it, Sculley told Isaacson. "I realized for the first time in four months that I couldn't say no," he said. He started at Apple the following Monday.

## Taking a Risk

I have a similar hiring story where I, too, rolled the dice and took a chance on a new hire that I thought could revolutionize our business.

In the advertising industry, you aren't taken seriously until you land a blue chip account—a Fortune 500 client. That relationship shapes how your agency is perceived, so winning a major account is critical for your long-term survival. The inability to win a blue chip account suggests to others that your work isn't good enough.

Knowing that our agency had to win a major account, I went looking for a business development pro who could bring one in for us—a "whale hunter." This person would have a big Rolodex and dozens of "ins" with major brands that we could tap into.

I found him.

Unfortunately, we couldn't afford him. He wanted a $350,000 salary plus commission to join our team. We didn't have it, but I knew for the business to survive, we couldn't go another day without him either. At the time we only had enough money in our bank account to pay him for six months. So my partner and I took a pay cut to be able to bring him on. This was a leap of faith that could have ended disastrously.

We rolled the dice. We were all in, for better or worse.

Fortunately, it was for better. That commitment paid off. Within 18 months our revenue had jumped by a factor of six thanks to his work. We were more than able to cover his salary, his commissions, and were scaling rapidly.

## Putting Muscle Behind Commitment

While everyone may want to be successful, a very small percentage will actually be willing to do the work required to make that happen. This is true whether we're talking about building a business, improving a personal relationship, or losing weight.

Let's take weight loss as an example of what I'm talking about. Sure, you may tell all your friends that you're going on a diet soon so you can lose those extra pounds you've added to your frame, but speaking it does not make it so. If you're truly committed to losing weight, you'll sign a year-long contract—none of this month-to-month stuff—at a gym and then you'll sign a six-month contract with a personal trainer who will meet with you several times a week to work out.

Once you've committed yourself financially to taking action, you are much more likely to follow through.

The truth is, commitment requires sacrifice. Depending on the type of commitment you're making, business or personal, your sacrifices will vary. If you're building a business, you may have to sacrifice money by reinvesting earnings back into the business, rather than in a hefty paycheck. You may have to sacrifice time with your family or give up planned vacations or trips. And you may have to sacrifice your health to some degree, giving up hours of sleep to spend on work or staying out of the gym while you put time into proposals and client work instead.

Commitment is bigger than just saying it. Commitment is more than words, it's about action, about taking a chance with no safety net in order to significantly improve your odds of success.

Promise me two years from now you're not having the same conversation about what could be because you've taken the chance and made the commitment.

## Speed Read

- Burn the ships around you to force you to take the action you need to. That means: Quitting your job, maxing out your credit cards and investing your savings to start your business, uprooting your family and selling your home, taking on a line of credit to buy a building for your company

- Burning the ships forces you to take real action and not turn back. It forces commitment to your goals.
- The faster you act, the sooner you'll see the results of your commitment—the sooner things can start to turn around.

# Create Alignment

Picture a huge Viking ship with rows and rows of strong men pushing huge oars through the water. The Vikings themselves are powering the ship, moving it forward with each stroke. The more in sync their oars, the faster and easier the ship moves toward its destination. However, if some rowers get out of sync—maybe they're tired or they misheard a command—the ship is going to stop dead in the water or merely circle. With people rowing in different directions, the Vikings are wasting precious energy and the ship is stalled.

That's exactly what happens when everyone in your business isn't aligned. Unless everyone, from your management team to your employees to your suppliers, partners, and clients, understands the direction your business is headed and what they can do to contribute, you're going nowhere fast.

It is critical to get your entire team aligned quickly in order to gain speed and scale. If you don't, you'll miss business opportunities, lose sales, and pass up strong hiring candidates while expenses will rise, productivity will fall, and you'll be effectively dead in the water.

Until you understand the who, what, when, why, and how of your business, it's impossible to achieve alignment.

## Believing in Your Sales Message

Alignment starts with your products and services. If everyone in your company doesn't believe in what you sell, they won't be effective in attracting customers. Everyone needs to be able to articulate how what you sell helps customers and why they should invest in it. If they can't, you'll be out of business quickly.

Your employees, partners, and customers need to be able to tell someone else what kind of product or service you deliver and how it will change the customer's life. That's really what it comes down to.

Think about the last time you asked for help from a company employee and they weren't able to demonstrate they understood your problem or knew how to solve it. (This recently happened for me at a home improvement chain.) That company probably lost you as a customer, didn't they? That's what you want to try and avoid.

It doesn't matter if your new herbal supplement cures cancer, if your people can't flat out say it, prove it, and believe it, your important discovery won't matter.

But your product or service doesn't have to save lives. Maybe you sell more mundane items like stand up paddleboards, bath towels, or shoes, or services like car washes, blog content, or professional photography. No matter what your company sells customers, everyone you work with needs to understand it and sing its praises.

We talk about "drinking the Kool-Aid" as an expression of the degree to which your employees believe in what you're selling. I want them to go from just drinking the Kool-Aid to swimming in it. They need to be all in. When that happens, your business growth becomes unstoppable.

## Recalibrate Regularly

One hundred years ago it was easy to get everyone aligned within a company. You had senior managers who would meet and decide on strategy and tactics and then meet with their direct reports to set goals, and then those direct reports would meet with the supervisors under them, etc. Word would quickly trickle down through the organization regarding priorities and expectations. In these command-and-control environments, there was no second guessing or pushback. People were aligned, or else.

Then again, external change was generally gradual and slow. Once a business was aligned it really wasn't necessary to reconvene and recalibrate for many months. Everyone knew their role and they performed.

Today, however, the marketplace is changing so fast, thanks to technology—moving at light speed—that if you're not sitting down almost daily with your partners and direct reports, it's likely you're no longer aligned. The speed of change requires that we recalibrate every morning, to ensure everyone is up to speed on market conditions, our priorities and objectives. If you don't check in and update everyone daily, you can easily shift course without realizing it. Then, only a few days later, you've lost ground.

New disrupters are forcing companies to constantly recalibrate. What I mean is that as businesses become aware of market changes, whether as a result of conditions such as new legislation, a competing product introduction, a new contract opportunity, or something else, management needs to sit down as a group and revisit their positions on the who, what, why, when, where, and how of the business.

I remember hearing in 2013 that there was a massive fire at Hynix, a memory chip factory in China. You wouldn't think that a fire in one plant on the other side of the world would have much of a ripple effect in the U.S., but it did. And the companies that recognized the situation quickly ended up much better off.

The problem with that fire at Hynix is that the company was the second-largest manufacturer of computer DRAM (dynamic random access memory) chips in the world, behind Samsung. It supplied one-third of the world's memory chips. The 90-minute blaze damaged the clean room, putting production back as much as six months, one industry expert estimated.

Almost immediately, the market price of DRAM chips rose from $1.60 each to $1.90 and would soon go higher. Computer and electronics manufacturers such as Apple, Dell, Sony, and Samsung that were relying on shipments of chips from Hynix that would not be coming had to quickly try and source chips from other sources. It was a mad scramble as companies tried to find chips to buy while, at the same time, not overspending on this one component.

I share this story simply to point out that your situation can change in an instant, sometimes by events you could never have predicted, so don't rely on occasional or even weekly team meetings to ensure that everyone's on the same page. Check in daily.

Here is when that one-page attack and conquer plan *really* becomes useful.

Your one-page plan is your road map and as your destination changes, or the route you're taking has to be detoured, whether due to a massive supplier fire or some other reason, your plan should be updated and shared.

## Agreement is Not Alignment

The bigger your company grows, the more important alignment is. And by alignment, I don't just mean agreement on a few points.

I learned this the hard way in my first business. My partner and I agreed on what our business was and what we were working toward but, unfortunately, we weren't truly aligned on what our business offered. It started out as a web development agency but quickly expanded beyond that because we were so money-hungry.

While we were selling website development, we would get requests from companies for other services, including SEO, logo design, brochure creation, and blog content curation. Sure, they were related services, but they were different enough that as we accepted more of these types of projects, we had to bring in additional talent to serve these customers. For example, website design and logo design require two different skillsets. The same is true of brochure creation and SEO— different skillsets.

So while this additional work certainly brought in revenue, it required that we add workers with the requisite skills in order to perform the work. Our costs increased. Then once these employees were on board, we had to continue to feed them with additional work to keep them busy, which meant that we had to start hunting for similar work that we originally hadn't planned on taking.

We quickly became focused on covering our fixed costs rather than on growing the business. We'd take on virtually any kind of project in the name of revenue generation.

That's not the way to scale with speed.

Unfortunately, this sent a mixed message to our team. What was the core business? It became less and less clear, to them and to us. What we were selling had expanded well beyond website development, while who we were selling to also became blurred.

Internally, there was a need for many more conversations about how to approach situations, since new ones were coming up more frequently. "Do you have a sec?" was a common question. Our efforts were scattered and fragmented and it showed.

What became clear, with 20/20 hindsight, is that the closer you are all aligned, the fewer questions come up about how to handle situations. Employees already know the answer because you've discussed it. Increased alignment reduces all that additional chatter and noise. It improves productivity and it reduces cost.

> *The marketplace is changing so fast, thanks to technology, that if you're not sitting down almost daily with your partners and direct reports, it's likely you're no longer aligned.*

## How to Get Aligned

Creating internal alignment starts with the 30,000-foot view of your company—what it is, who it serves, what it sells, why, how it benefits customers, and under what situations customers typically need your products or services. That's your one-page plan, in a nutshell.

Refer back to your one-page plan as your road map.

Then break that larger plan down into 90-day plans with associated goals. Where do you want to be at the end of each quarter with respect to clients, revenue, head count, and other metrics that impact your business?

From there, break the 90-day plans down into monthly plans for each team.

Then take it down to the level of the individual employee. What should they be working on this week and this month to support their team's goals, which roll into the company's quarterly and annual goals? They should be clear. You should make it clear to them.

Employees should be able to articulate:

- The goals they are currently working to meet.
- What the company's expectations of them are and how their performance will be measured.

- What rewards are available for consistent successful achievement of their goals, including compensation and career path.
- The possible punishment they will receive if they fail to perform, such as demotion or firing.

I discovered the importance of alignment at a company I joined, where there was no plan or alignment. Everyone was doing their own thing in support of what they thought the company's core mission was. While they may have been working toward a goal, they were not aligned and there was a lot of wasted energy.

Realizing that everyone needed to be aligned, I introduced the planning process, beginning with the one-page plan and filtering it down to every employee. With everyone then working toward one common goal, with specific deliverables and measurable expectations, we achieved between 30 and 60 percent year-over-year growth for the next few years.

## Avoiding the Deadly Habits

In order to get everyone aligned, there also needs to be an agreement about what behaviors will *not* be tolerated. These are four to eight deadly habits that are detrimental and won't allow you to scale with speed. Any team member that consistently shows these behaviors must be fired. They are toxic. They are a cancer. You must remove them.

You know what your goals are, you know what you need to do, and the pace at which you need to work, based on your one-page attack and conquer plan. Now it's time to evaluate your organization and culture to spot the negative habits that are kills your company's progress and growth.

For example, at one of my last companies we'd routinely talk in bullshit; conversations were circular and we never got anything done. Or we'd always start sentences with, "We can't because..." Everything was insurmountable. I knew that we had to remove that phrase and that thinking from our culture in order to scale with speed.

We also had become complacent and had a tolerance for mediocrity. When someone finally turned something in, okay became okay enough. Lack of accountability with the failure to deliver on time was another killer.

I knew these behaviors and habits had to change in order to grow a profitable business I could ultimately sell. Which we did. Part of that process requires you to remove people from the organization, retrain others, and find new ones that are aligned with the new direction and pace of the business. Never be scared to remove someone. There's an unlimited number of people you can replace them with.

To spot your company's deadly habits:

- Look for clues regarding poor performance, slow delivery, and mediocre results. These are symptoms of your deadly habits.
- Find evidence. Look for proof that these are your major problems, that they are prohibiting the achievement of your goals.
- Write out the cure. Brainstorm the solution to eradicating this behavior.
- Identify qualities and skills needed. What behaviors will turn the situation around?

Once you've identified your deadly habits and the antidote, you need to inform the organization and empower each employee to hold others accountable. Have visual cues around your workspace that manifest into action. Post reminders of these deadly habits in conference rooms and on the walls so that when anyone exhibits this behavior, others can feel empowered to respectfully call them on it.

Having reminders posted publicly gives everyone permission to point out the unwanted behaviors.

| The Deadly 7 Habits | Evidence | Cure | Quality and Skills Needed |
|---|---|---|---|
| Talking In Bullshit | Sugarcoated conversations<br><br>Failure to deliver bad news | Transparency<br><br>Tell the truth even when ugly | Clear, concise communication<br><br>Giving and receiving feedback<br><br>Dealing with defensiveness |
| Living In Quicksand | Live in the fog<br><br>Unclear owners and roles<br><br>Too many downstream vetoes and second guessing | Clarity<br><br>Accountability<br><br>Trust your partners | Orientation towards action<br><br>Goal setting<br><br>Effective meetings<br><br>Ability to commit<br><br>Accountability |
| Need For Certainty | Cud Chewing<br><br>Spinning<br><br>Wasting time & resources | Confidence in your ability<br><br>Make decisions @ 70% | Trust<br><br>Confidence<br><br>Freedom to fail |
| Participation In Game Of Thrones | Us vs. them<br><br>Triangles | No "I" in team | High trust leadership<br><br>Collaborative<br><br>Decision making |

| The Deadly 7 Habits | Evidence | Cure | Quality and Skills Needed |
|---|---|---|---|
| "We Can't Because" | Negativity<br><br>Leading with NO<br><br>Focus on roadblocks | Answer yes and find a way<br><br>Optimism<br><br>Make it happen attitude | Positivity<br><br>Ability to zoom |
| Tolerance For Mediocrity | Low standards<br><br>Good enough is good enough | Define new standards<br><br>Nothing less than great | Manager that manage differently |
| Failure To Deliver | Not doing what you say you will<br><br>Dropping the ball<br><br>Letting each other down | Ownership<br><br>Measurement<br><br>Accountability | Accountable teammates<br><br>Regular, meaningful feedback |

*These are the deadly habits we identified at one of my past companies. To get a blank copy for yourself, visit JudgeGraham.com.*

## Alignment as a Hiring Tool

If you can be crystal clear about what a job is and what it isn't and what the expectations are for a new employee at the outset, you have a much better chance of finding a candidate who will come in aligned. They will already understand the company's goals and how they can play a part.

People want to be led. They want to be shown how what they're doing is contributing to the company's success—how it impacts the company on a daily basis. Purpose is important, especially to Millennial and Gen Z workers. So when you explain what their purpose is and how they can make a difference, engagement and retention skyrockets.

But alignment isn't buy-in. You can't make everyone happy or force them to agree with the direction you're taking the company or the decisions you're making. Not everyone will. But they do need to respect the decision and support it. They need to be willing to give their best effort in support of the direction you're taking the business.

## Speed Read

- Making sure everyone connected with your business understands what you do, why you do it, when (under what circumstances) customers need what you sell, who your target market is, and how they use it and benefit from it is critical for getting everyone aligned and working toward the same objective.

- To spot your company's deadly habits: 1) Look for clues regarding poor performance, slow delivery, and mediocre results, 2) find evidence 3) write out the cure 4) identify qualities and skills needed.

- Your one-page plan should be starting point for all other planning and goal-setting within the company. Your plan sets the large goal, which can then be broken down by business unit, team, and individual employee. Employees don't have to necessarily agree with the goals you've set to be in alignment, but they do need to support them.

- Have daily meetings, even if only for 10-15 minutes, to share new information about the market and the company and to recalibrate expectations within your team.

# Team Culture

Now that everyone's aligned in the direction you want to go, with expectations set and understood, and you're moving at the speed you want to operate at, it's time to build a culture around that alignment.

There's no way you can achieve a rapid growth trajectory if you're the one doing all the work. Sure, a team of independent contractors, rather than employees, can work, but only if you can get them all aligned. That's tougher to do when you're managing people who don't rely totally on you for their income; by definition, independent contractors cannot be employees and need to do work for other clients.

Your team should consist of like-minded people who know what's expected of them. They know their job and are committed to doing their best. They understand the company's mission and are in support of it. They know how they'll be rewarded if their performance helps the company achieve its goals and they also know what the repercussions are for not performing as expected.

Clarity is important, but so is freedom. Your employees need to be trusted to do their jobs to the best of their ability the way that they think they should be done. If you feel the need to micromanage, to instruct employees on every aspect of their job, then you have the wrong people in place. You need to empower them to work independently.

That said, giving them guard rails, or parameters, isn't a bad thing. You can convey that you support them and are available if they need help with statements such as:

- "I'll check back on your progress tomorrow."
- "Here are some resources you may want to use."
- "Let me know if you run into any issues with X."

You can have safeguards in place to prevent employees from going too far astray without hovering over them. Besides, you don't have time for that.

Once you have your tribe in place, your ability to scale with speed comes down to execution.

### Building a Positive Corporate Culture

Of course, if you discover that there are people on your team who aren't rowing in the same direction, you need to remove them. There's nothing more damaging to your culture than people who are not aligned with what you're doing and the pace at which you're working.

And there's nothing worse for team performance than toxic personalities—people who complain, who gossip about co-workers or leaders, who question the company's strategy or tactics, and who generally make your workplace uncomfortable. You can't afford to have people on your team who are not focused on the work to be done and how they can best contribute.

I speak from experience on this one. At one of my companies we had a member of the senior leadership team who wasn't aligned with the direction we were headed. He was afraid of change, noncommittal when it came to voicing support for our direction, and expressed negativity behind the backs of other leaders. Now, you know that when you have someone overseeing 30 people that his views are very likely to cascade down through his team. So instead of one non-believer, we then had 31.

Since he was a senior manager, I spent hours with him over the course of several weeks trying to address his skepticism and explain our strategy for the future. I wanted his buy-in but, more importantly, I needed him accept what we were doing and support the work. He couldn't. I met with his team, trying to get them aligned and to re-energize them because, at that point, they were a negative bunch amidst an otherwise positive, optimistic crew. The difference was stark.

They were resistant to change and loyal to their leader. He had created a fiefdom within the organization and was reluctant to cooperate.

I could see he was unwilling to change. So I let him go.

I had put so much time and energy into trying convince one person on my team to work with us, not against us, and he just didn't want to. Our progress stalled. We couldn't scale or achieve complete alignment with him on staff.

Once he was fired, I had to let an additional five members of his team go as well because they remained true to the culture he had established, which was not in line with what we wanted for the company as a whole.

Building culture is tough. Not everyone will embrace it and some will leave or be asked to leave if it becomes apparent they aren't willing to support the new direction or environment.

Scale and speed only happen when everyone's rowing in the same direction. Otherwise, you're stuck in neutral as competitors pass you by.

## Communicating Clear Opportunities

Once you have the right people on your team, you need to do all you can to reinforce the company's mission and growth strategy and support them as professionals.

Make everything about creating and delivering results for your customers. That's your central focus. Then, once everyone is working toward that objective, think about how you can help your employees grow and build skills. The more capable they are of serving your customers, the faster your business can grow.

There are two aspects to providing opportunities to your team:

- Investing in their professional development
- Eliminating processes that interfere with their work

Since a happier staff delivers at higher levels, you want to make sure you're doing all you can to communicate the opportunities for growth and development to your employees. What could their future look like at your company? If there isn't much room for advancement, their time under your roof is likely to be short-lived. That doesn't mean that you have to create annual promotion opportunities, but do think about what you can do to help them build skills if they're not advancing through the hierarchy. That might include:

- A formal mentoring program where junior employees are paired with senior employees to create advocacy relationships and help them learn how to further their careers.
- Paying for an external mentoring or coaching program, especially if your company is smaller and has fewer senior level positions.
- Tuition reimbursement for advanced degrees.

- An annual professional development budget for each employee to spend on industry conferences, workshops, and trade fairs.
- Outlining a potential career path for each employee, based on achieving certain performance metrics and experience.
- Articulating specific compensation increases and bonus opportunities based on the success of the company; sometimes called a long-term incentive plan.

In addition to helping employees picture spending their career at your company, help them in the short-term by eliminating obstacles to their performance. This might include:

- Simplifying approval processes to hasten progress.
- Providing the authority to make decisions under a certain dollar amount.
- Involving them in management meetings, to get a sense of how decisions are made and to have the opportunity to provide input.
- Rewarding suggestions made to simplify or improve internal processes.

Make it in everyone's best interests to hasten progress and reduce roadblocks and you'll be surprised by what you can achieve. As they say, what gets rewarded gets done.

*Scale and speed only happen when everyone's rowing in the same direction.*

## Create Visual Reminders of Your Core Values
Once you get everyone aligned, it's easier to keep them aligned when you provide regular reminders of your core values. These reminders

should be shared internally and externally, to reinforce what you stand for and are working for, whether that's the ultimate customer experience, the latest technology for your home, or the simplest tax preparation service ever.

Articulate what your business does for its customers and then translate that into a slogan and graphics that reinforce it. Then, plaster them everywhere. Some ideas for where they should appear include:

- T-shirts
- Your website
- Murals or wall hangings
- Pens and pencils
- Social media posts
- Your newsletter
- Signage

I have been known to create murals that I have applied to the walls to remind employees why we were at work. It was also a way to convey to visiting customers what our number one priority was.

Creating a core message and communicating it to everyone helps reinforce the culture you're trying to build.

## The Benefits of a Positive Corporate Culture

Fostering an environment that inspires people to do their best work and to have fun creates a culture that people want to be part of. When they know their work is appreciated and valued, and that's reflected in their compensation, the attitude of employees is positive and optimistic. And when you take the time to recognize hard workers, even if their efforts are behind the scenes and not evident to common observers, you can establish a bond that leads to loyalty and dedication.

Culture can pay off big in terms of employee performance and retention. A Columbia University study found that companies with a positive, or "rich," corporate culture had likely job turnover of 13.9 percent, while companies with a poor or negative culture had likely turnover of 48.4 percent. Simply put, employees want to stick around when the environment within an organization is supportive and encouraging; they're quick to leave when it's not.

Turnover, of course, is expensive and interferes with your ability to scale with speed.

That was the case at one company I owned. Early on, when we didn't have much of a culture, we had turnover that exceeded 30 percent. It was hard to make much progress because as soon as we trained someone new, someone else left. We were merely treading water.

But after investing time in articulating the type of people we wanted and what we were all working toward, we started to get some traction. We developed a culture and demonstrated to our team that we valued them. In response, we got 98 percent retention. People didn't leave and we won "Best Place to Work" honors multiple times. That's when things really started to click.

You'll never achieve real growth if you don't have a solid culture that attracts more star performers and holds onto the ones you have, and that gives them the chance to grow professionally along the way.

### Speed Read

- Hire the right people and give them the freedom to do their jobs the best way they know how. Trying to micromanage or oversee their every move belittles them, crushes their confidence, and makes for an unhappy culture.
- Let toxic personalities go asap. People who aren't aligned with the company's values will wreak havoc and slow your progress.

- Invest in programs that help employees expand their skills, learn from more senior staff members, and have the chance to network within their field or your industry. Providing professional development opportunities increases loyalty and appreciation for your business, which creates a positive culture.

# Get into Flow

Y ou need alignment and rhythm within your company to make real progress. With your team aligned and a culture of urgency built around results and speed, it's possible to achieve peak performance by getting into flow.

You have business habits just as you have personal habits. They include things like how many times you check email a day, whether you're more likely to text than pick up a phone, the path you take to the vending machine, and what time you leave for work. They're part of the rhythm of your day, just as when you grab that first cup of coffee is part of your routine or when you first look at your calendar.

Habits are important, especially when you're trying to achieve exponential growth at breakneck speed. They are a form of practice, a way of trying to gain control over your schedule and your regimen. They're also a way to prepare for the unexpected.

## Focusing on Priorities

One thing I had every employee in my companies do daily was to create a written plan, their Money Sheet. It was an outline of what they were going to accomplish that day—what they were going to focus on. They used it to focus at least 75 percent of their time on revenue-generating tasks.

The plans varied by department and by person. For example, in sales, some days the focus might be on customer outreach. There might be a target number of phone calls listed on a daily plan. But in marketing, the focus that same day might be on completing a bid or proposal for new business. In the IT department, the focus might be testing a new SEO tool we had discovered, or making progress on a new website feature we had in development.

Everyone's daily plan was different, reflecting their varied roles within the company, but I expected everyone to prepare one. And I checked in on them to confirm that they'd done it and to make sure it was aligned with the company's larger goals. I didn't want people investing hours on a task that really wasn't critical for our growth; that would be wasteful.

So I walked the halls every morning, hoping to encourage the habit of preparing a daily plan the first thing in the morning. I'm 6 feet tall and 250 pounds and I wear cowboy boots. When I decided everyone had had enough time to fill out their daily plan, I would start making my rounds. Employees could hear the click-clack of my heels as my boots traveled the hardwoods to check in with everyone and knew they'd better get their plans done asap.

Some people might read that and think I was a micro-manager, always wanting to look over my employees' daily plans. I don't think I was. I was helping them to create a new habit—a habit that would make or break the company. I was being a leader, a coach and nudging them to determine their highest priorities and focus on them, to the exclusion of all other tasks. And by walking the halls in the morning, I made sure everyone knew they had a deadline to get those daily plans written up.

## Developing a Rhythm

Checking in with everyone was one way that I created an internal rhythm inside the company. Employees knew that sometime between 9:00 am and 10:00 every day, I would stop by their doorway or cube to ask how it was going.

Another part of that daily rhythm was the 8:49 am standing meeting—meaning that we stood for it, not sat in chairs—I held with our leadership team. We'd stand in a loose circle every morning and review issues that had come up the previous day and discuss how best to handle them, as well as confirm priorities for that day. Then each department head would go and hold a similar standing meeting with their employees, to be sure everyone was rowing in the same direction and focused on the same priorities.

By starting the day with a kind of priority reset, we could all feel confident that we were working on the right tasks and that we were operating in sync, in alignment. Without those regular check-ins, it's very possible that everyone could be productive yet completing tasks that really didn't need to be done. I wanted to avoid that.

We also had mandatory Monday all-hands meetings to confirm the key initiatives for the week, to confirm everyone had set the right priorities and focus in support of those initiatives. And we'd review our successes from the prior week.

Quarterly agency updates, which were also all-hands meetings, communicated to everyone how we performed against our 90-day goals and how we've course-corrected, if needed, to continue to improve that performance in the coming 90 days.

When you're in rhythm, in flow, you know it. You can feel it. You know what you're expected to do and you can adjust slightly if you noticed that you're out of sync with others on your team.

As I say that, I picture a middle school band trying to play together. You could have some excellent musicians on the stage and yet, if they weren't all watching the conductor, they would still sound shitty. That's the difference that rhythm makes—beautiful music versus a cacophony of different instruments being played at various tempos.

The same is true of rowers in crew, especially in eight-man boats. From the outside it just looks like eight people rowing simultaneously to make the boat speed ahead faster than another. In reality, there's a lot more than goes into making the boat move. Explains former collegiate rower Bruce Eckfeldt:

"…everyone must work together to balance the boat and have exact timing. Your hands must be at exactly the right height as you slide up to the catch. Every oar has to drop into the water at the exact same time. Everyone needs to pull at equal pressure. All the blades need to come out of the water and release in unison. Any deviation disrupts the boat."

To achieve optimal speed, rowers, like businesses, need to achieve balance and flow. A rhythm of everyone working in perfect harmony.

## Getting into Flow

Rhythm and flow are similar, but different. Rhythm has more to with our routines—routines that we work hard to sync with others, so that we are in alignment at work, while flow has to do with our mental state. Flow is "that moment when creativity and productivity sprung from your mind smoothly," says Mihaly Csikszentmihalyi, the father of flow. It's that feeling when you're in the zone, when you lose a sense of time and your work becomes effortless. Flow makes peak performance possible. It's what you want every employee to get to.

Both rhythm and flow are needed to be successful at scaling with speed—rhythm to get in sync with the rest of your team and flow to be able to achieve more in less time.

When you're in flow, you are super focused about what you need to get done. You have better decision-making ability and can more easily see the possible solutions. Work progress comes easily. You're at peace, not stressed, and yet the answers come quickly. You're having fun and achieving optimal productivity.

If only you could harness this mental state…

You can. Sometimes flow arrives unexpectedly, but there are steps you can take to make the experience of flow more likely to occur:

- **Choose a task you really need to get done**. It's best if you're not super stressed about the approaching deadline for completion and maybe even looking forward to working on it. Activities with a creative element are often a good choice. In fact, Steven Kotler reported that, "In our studies at the Flow Genome Project, people are reporting a 500 percent to 700 percent boost in creativity in flow."
- **Make sure it's challenging work and not just paper-pushing**. The work you need to get done should be mentally stimulating. Perhaps there's a problem you need to solve or a new idea you need to prepare and present.
- **Start work at a time during the day when you're usually at your best**. Morning people should tackle this first while night owls may find that mid-day or afternoon are when they're really on their game. Go with your biorhythms.

- **Find a quiet place.** Turn off your phone, lock your door, shut down email notifications and zero in on the task at hand. Try and limit interruptions as much as possible. One study found that 87 workplace interruptions are typical during a work day. That's a lot of stopping and starting what you're working on.

- **Focus solely on what you need to complete.** Try hard not to let your mind wander. Stay focused on your challenge. Push yourself to come up with new answers, new ideas.

- **Stop work only when you become distracted or unable to make more progress.** Part of the challenge is pushing your mind into new places, forcing it to stretch and make new connections. That takes practice, so work as long as you can and then move on.

The time and energy saved when you're in flow is significant. You can achieve so much more in much less time and with much less energy. Concentration and motivation are at their peak when you're in flow. Flow can be fuel for scaling with speed.

*Flow is "that moment when creativity and productivity sprung from your mind smoothly."*

You'll be amazed at how much more productive you can be when you're in flow. Jamie Wheal, executive director of The Flow Genome Project, reports that "studies run by the U.S. military and Advanced Brain Monitoring figured out that snipers in flow learn 200 percent to 500 percent faster than normal." Even if you could achieve a 50 percent or 100 percent improvement in productivity, imagine the impact that would have on your business.

The thing about flow and rhythm is that it's immediately apparent when you have it and when you don't. With flow, you can work at an individual level or organizational. Rhythm requires other people.

And when employees are all in flow, the potential improvement in productivity is immense. Not only that, they'll be more engaged, more fulfilled, happier, and more positive. The sky's the limit in terms of what you can accomplish together.

### Speed Read

- Rhythm is working in sync with other employees. Coordinating efforts so that you're working in concert is key to being able to scale with speed. If some employees are out of sync, you'll never make as much headway.

- A flow state occurs when you're in the zone, when work is effortless and fun. You lose track of time and are able to accomplish so much more—often breakthrough work— without even trying.

- To get into flow, choose a task you really need to get done, make sure it's challenging work and not just paper-pushing, start work at a time of day when you're usually at your best, find a quiet place, focus solely on what you need to complete, stop work only when you become distracted or are unable to make more progress.

# Speed Retention

"How important is corporate culture? It's everything," says Liz Ryan, author of *Reinvention Roadmap: Break the Rules to Get the Job You Want and Career You Deserve*. This is spot on and the leaders that recognize this are the ones winning in the marketplace.

You have to build the culture and then have the process and rules to make people love working there. If you're constantly replacing people, you can't move with speed. I don't care if you're in service or selling widgets, without great people, you'll never have a great company. Great people want to work for great companies. Customers want to buy products and services from great companies, and great companies are the most sought after.

No matter what type of business you're in—manufacturing, product sales, or service—you're really selling the skills of your people.

Their talents and expertise are what are going to sell your customers, so try and land the best ones. Become the preferred supplier in your industry, whatever that is. Fill your team with lackluster recruits and you'll have a hard time creating a competitive advantage and an even harder time scaling.

Then when you're successful in attracting the best in the business, hold onto them!

It's expensive when employees decide to leave. Employee Benefit News reported that it costs 33 percent of an employee's compensation to replace them. And when the median salary for a college-educated worker is $62,036, as of 2014, according to the Bureau of Labor Statistics, that means you're spending a good $20,000 every time a professional-level employee walks—more if they're a top earner.

It will be hard to scale with speed if you're constantly spending money trying to find new employees, not to mention the time it takes to onboard and train them to do their jobs.

It makes more sense to invest even a portion of that money you would spend recruiting new people on retaining the great employees you've already spent time and money attracting and training. Once you have them as part of your team, you need to take care of them.

### Be Transparent

That starts with clear communication with them. People can't perform to their abilities unless they understand the company's mission—how is it helping people, what their individual role and purpose is, and how they'll be rewarded for giving it their all.

Share your financials—with everyone internally—so that they can better understand how the business works and how their efforts support its success or failure. Explain where the company is financially, what the goals are, and how you'll achieve them with their hard work. Then outline how they'll benefit. Tell them, essentially, "These are our expectations. If we hit these target numbers, this is what it will mean for you." Of course, the reward could be a one-time bonus, a raise, a piece of the company, or a company trip to the Bahamas. You decide what will motivate your team the most—asking them for feedback is always smart—and see what you can do to give it to them.

You'll want to involve your human resource (HR) team if you're large enough to have a designated HR rep, to help in creating career development plans for everyone. Each employee needs to understand where they fit in and how you can help them grow and develop into more senior roles. If you want them around long-term, show them that you have a plan that will give them promotions and raises. Demonstrate your commitment to them and you'll be much more likely to get a commitment in return.

Then always keep your eye out for great people. Don't wait until you have an opening to start scouring other companies for top candidates. Keep your employees on alert for strong performers and reward them for referrals that turn into new hires. Develop a database of people you'd like to have on your team, tell them that, and then stay in touch until an appropriate opening occurs. Or, if they're that good, create a role for them so the opportunity to hire them doesn't slip away.

 *"How important is corporate culture? It's everything."*

### Create Happy Employees

Once you've found rock stars, do your best to keep them. This means anticipating their needs and meeting them. That could include a wide range of perks and benefits, including:

- **Equipment**. Find out what your employees need, or even would like, to be more productive. That could be a computer upgrade every two years, a company cell phone, or even a treadmill desk. In one of my companies some employees wanted the option to work at a standing desk, so we provided them.

- **Training**. This could be a regular, monthly internal training day or money allocated to each employee to allow them to stay current or get ahead in their field. Support of their professional development is crucial. Offering tuition reimbursement for employees who want to earn an advanced degree is also a big draw. Even Walmart is now offering to pay for some of its employees' college degrees.

- **Time away from the office**. No matter what your industry, it's important to give employees their personal time and space. Offer ample vacation weeks and extra days as needed.

- **Maternity and paternity leave**. Having a baby is stressful for employees, so giving them time to be with their new addition can cement that employer-employee bond like you wouldn't believe. While paid time off is, obviously, preferred from an employee perspective, even just the option to take time off at reduced or no pay is helpful.

- **Flexible work**. Depending on your industry, this may be easier for some than others, but try and allow employees to decide where they can work. Sure, you may need people at the office regularly, but allowing two to three days of work from home can be a lifesaver for some workers. The same with hours; does it really matter if someone works from 7 a.m. to 3 p.m. or 10 to 6? That ability to control their schedule is everything to some employees.

- **Job security**. Employees frequently worry about holding onto their jobs, especially in difficult situations, such as needing to be home for a few weeks to care for a sick kid or recovering from their own injury. Employees feel more valued when they don't have to worry about their job if they or someone in their family becomes ill. Make it clear that their job is there for them. The reduced stress alone from that reassurance is likely to earn you a loyal employee for life.

- **Support**. Sometimes employees hit a rough patch at home. Offering emotional and tangible support is another way to let them they are valued and that you care. That could be anything from organizing daily meal delivery while someone is grieving, providing Uber or Lyft credits to ensure they have transportation, or just checking in by phone to see how they're doing.

- **Recognition**. This is a big one, and it doesn't have to cost you a cent. Take time to regularly recognize people who are doing a good job. Walk around and have conversations about what they're doing and let them know you really appreciate their work. Whenever you can, publicly show appreciation for the great workers on your team. Call them out by name and mention what they did that was so valuable for the company. Consider handing out plaques or trophies—people love tangible reminders of that recognition. Mainly, let employees know that you're paying attention and that you know they're doing a terrific job.

Of course, paying competitive salaries and offering health insurance are also smart ways to show employees they are valued. That doesn't mean you have to throw money at them, though. It turns out, employees are more likely to leave due to a perceived lack of career opportunities at your company than due to low compensation, a Ranstad USA study found.

## Infuse Fun

Don't overlook opportunities to make your workplace more enjoyable for everyone. The fact is, studies have shown that happy employees are more productive—20 percent more, according to one report. Fortunately, making them happy doesn't have to cost a lot, but offering extras can go a long way toward keeping your best people:

- **Food**. We would frequently have lunch meetings catered for our team. Not only did this ensure they got a free meal, but then they could keep working on client projects. This was much appreciated during crunch times.
- **A place to de-stress**. In one company, I created a yoga room where employees could go do yoga throughout the day as needed. You could bring in fitness pros at lunch to offer a workout or give employees free memberships to a nearby gym.
- **Pets at work**. This used to be unusual, but today many companies—large and small—allow dogs at work. Cats may be welcome, too, but I've really only heard about dogs. Allowing pets to come to work reduces the need for employees to run home to let them out and, let's face it, having animals around helps reduce everyone's stress.
- **Entertainment**. Some companies schedule fun internal contests to engage people. It could be a cooking contest, for example, your own version of a tough mudder competition, a Halloween costume event, or something else designed to provide a break from a work and a smile or laugh.
- **Milestone reward**. When employees have invested several years at the company, some business owners offer a reward. It's a carrot to stick around, and it seems to work well. Samantha Martin of Media Maison in New York offers employees who reach a three-year anniversary a trip anywhere in the world;

one employee just got back from Paris, reported a *New York Times* article. Other companies, such as Bain and McKinsey offer sabbaticals.

Keep in mind that this isn't the complete list of any perk you could offer your employees. These are things I've done and that I know of, but your team may have interests that you can meet that aren't on here.

For example, there's a consulting firm I know of that has been working like mad for a few months, so the president invited everyone and their spouses on a Caribbean cruise to help them relax. Granted, that's an expensive trip, but the business has been growing so fast that it can afford it. But maybe your team would love to go to Coachella, or a local concert. Maybe they'd like housing help—getting an advance to put down first and last month's rent. If you're in a major city, giving them paid monthly subway passes could be a godsend. Maybe they could use a free bike to get them to work. Be creative. And ask your team—what would make their day?

## Zappos as Culture Role Model

I'm sure you've heard stories about Zappos, the online shoe store, and its leader Tony Hsieh. The company hires slowly, places a premium on culture fit—it's 50 percent of the initial evaluation—and then invests in its people to hold onto them. But it also makes sure people are where they want to be. After an initial training period in its call center, employees are offered $3,000 to quit. Zappos wants them to stay, but if they're not happy, $3,000 is probably enough enticement to get them to move on.

Those who stay are shown what it's going to take to progress at Zappos. The company is very clear about what each employee needs to do to earn promotions and raises—and it's not based on subjective evaluations. Raises are based on skill-building. Master a skill associated with success in your job, pass a test, and you'll earn more money.

Performance evaluations, however, are done with respect to fit within the Zappos culture. Is your work and behavior a reflection of the company's 10 core values? The more it is, the more quickly you'll progress.

But there's a fun side to Zappos too. When employees finish training they have a graduation ceremony complete with pomp and circumstance and their whole team and family cheering them on. As part of their training, they compete in a scavenger hunt to learn more about the company. Apparently the cowbell features prominently in daily activity at the company (not sure why).

The goal at Zappos is to ensure customers are blown away by their shopping experience and to do that, company management understands that they have to have happy employees who are committed to providing that experience.

If your plan is to grow a monster business like Zappos, you need to accept that it's a team sport. If you don't take care of your team, you'll never win. You're only as good as your people.

**Speed Read**

- You won't be able to scale or grow without the efforts of your team. Investing in their happiness and satisfaction will reap productivity improvements of up to 20 percent and reduced turnover, which can quickly cost you tens of thousands of dollars.
- Sure, money makes a difference to employees, but not as much as other factors, such as feeling valued and appreciated. Recognize and reward employees as much as possible to solidify their continued employment.
- Don't forget to have fun. Employees who have fun at work, who look forward to going, will become super performers. So give them free meals every once in a while, hold funny competitions,

and give them more control over their jobs. Take care of them as if they were family.

# Part 5

# Dominate Your Top Priorities

*"Success requires massive action."*
**– Judge Graham**

Now that everything's in order, it's time to put the pedal to the medal. You need to 10x your actions - meaning expend 10 times the energy and resources - against your top priorities and head toward the path of full financial freedom.

Just remember, results happen in the work. This section is all about dominating in speed and action in order to be successful.

With everyone aligned and working to achieve your top priorities, stay focused. It's easy to become bored or complacent and shift your attention to new initiatives and strategies. Don't. Stick with what's working. Refine what you're currently doing to get better, but don't divert your attention to something new.

Keep your customers satisfied, too—they will make or break your business. If they love doing business with you their customer lifetime value will skyrocket and ensure your long-term success. If they feel like you don't care anymore, you'll lose them and your revenue will decline significantly. Make sure you take good care of your customers.

Use tools and systems to take the company's temperature regularly. You'll only know if you're hitting your targets or if you're off-course if you're routinely testing and monitoring your results.

# Focus at Least 75 Percent of Your Time on Revenue Generation

Revenue is the life blood of every business. Without it, you have no business. So focusing at least 75 percent of your time on revenue generation is critical if you want to scale to become a massive business. You'll be more productive and your company will make more money.

I've said it before and I'll say it again, scaling with speed requires hyper focus. Spreading your attention across a million tasks and priorities will get you nowhere. To progress and succeed quickly, you need to invest your time, money, and energy into revenue-generating activities. Period.

Of course, that requires knowing which of your activities is revenue-generating and likely to have the biggest payoff. Constantly scanning incoming emails, reading social media posts, and scouring property listings for the day when you'll be ready to buy your own commercial building are unlikely to have any material effect on your business growth today. Or even tomorrow. In fact, the impact is more likely to be negative, because you're not advancing your business with those activities. They are, pure and simple, time wasters.

On the other hand, researching hot prospects, typing up a new business proposal, and sending out a customer newsletter will spark positive growth. Of course, those kinds of tasks are harder and are often things people really don't love to do. There aren't many entrepreneurs who love to cold call but the successful ones do it anyway, because they understand it's the only way to grow.

### The Money Sheet

One way I quickly clear away the non-essential tasks on my to-do list is to create what I call a Money Sheet. It's a list of the six to eight highest priorities—the things I have to accomplish *today* to get closer to my monthly revenue goal.

The two biggest pieces of information on this sheet are 1) the monthly revenue goal and 2) the current balance needed — the difference — to reach the monthly goal.

For example, if you're running a sales group, you can walk around and look at each person's money sheet and recognize those who are ahead of the game. It makes performance a public measure within the organization.

Prioritize the top six to eight activities that will get you closer to achieving or exceeding your monthly revenue target. It doesn't matter if those priorities take you two hours or 24, you *must* complete them before you leave today in order for the money sheet to be successful.

- On any given day, my Money Sheet could have things on it like:
- Have lunch with a key client or referral source

**Stay Focused and Don't Finish Your Day Until All Items on Your Money Sheet Are Done!**
*Make It Happen!*

Monthly Revenue Goal:

Current Amount Needed to Reach Monthly Goal:

Fill out your top 6-8 priorities that you can complete today that get you closer to hitting your monthly revenue target.

1

2

3

4

5

6

7

8

JudgeGraham.com

*For a copy of a blank Money Sheet, go to JudgeGraham.com.*

- Make 100 cold calls
- Finalize copy for our new website
- Send out bids for new work

- Review client work about to be delivered
- Submit awards applications
- Post job opening

These were the high impact tasks that would have a direct impact in the short- and long-term on the company's success. Some were five minute items and others might take a few hours, but they were the keys to unlocking more opportunities for us.

My goal was to spend 75 percent of my day completing the tasks on my Money Sheet. In an eight-hour day, that meant that six hours were spent on these—proactive action items. The other two hours were spent on administrative activities that needed to be done but were more maintenance tasks than business growth opportunities, such as paying bills or responding to those never-ending emails and texts. These are the more reactive to-dos, in that someone else has often initiated them and is waiting for you to finish them.

The remaining 25 percent of your day should be spent on tasks that may still be critical to the ultimate success of your company, but they're not revenue-generating. They have little to no impact on the bottom line. These managerial or administrative tasks include things like:

- Conducting employee performance reviews
- Reviewing creative campaigns for your company
- Approving expense reports or payments
- Holding meetings with senior leadership
- Returning phone calls that came in during the day

These tasks still have to get done, but not first. These non-revenue-generating activities need to be squeezed in after you cross off everything on your money sheet. They can't be your first priority or you'll go out of business, but you also can't ignore them or your business will become really inefficient and poorly managed.

The money sheet isn't so much a to-do list as a hyper-focused list of revenue-generating activities that will propel you toward your goals. In fact, you won't reach your goals unless you shift your approach to your to-do items. Because many, if not most, of the things on your current to-do list really shouldn't be done at all, or should be done by someone else.

### How to Approach Daily Planning

To get the most out of your day, take some time at the end of each work day or first-thing in the morning to map out what you'll accomplish during the next work day. Block off obligations like meetings that you must attend and then fill in, in 30-minute blocks, what you'll focus on. Your schedule then might look something like this:

| 8:30  | Review calendar |
|-------|-----------------|
| 9:00  | Staff meeting |
| 9:30  | Review Acme Inc. business proposal |
| 10:00 | Meeting with legal about trademark |
| 10:30 | Interview CFO candidate |
| 11:00 | Call bank about increasing line of credit |
| 11:30 | Call Bob at Carrier re: bid; Call Susan at Google re: proposal |
| 12:00 | Lunch with mentee |
| 12:30 | Review website SEO report and approve changes to campaign |
| 1:00  | Call Angie at IBM to check in; Call Cheryl at Blue Cross Blue Shield |
| 1:30  | Call Tom at Target; Call Frank at Facebook |

| | |
|---|---|
| 2:00 | Prepare bid for Mercedes project |
| 2:30 | Prepare bid for Mercedes project |
| 3:00 | Study brief on NASCAR for meeting |
| 3:30 | Meeting with NASCAR about project |
| 4:00 | Meeting with NASCAR about project |
| 4:30 | Planning for next day |
| 5:00 | Drinks and dinner with client |

Your tasks will look different, of course, depending on your business, but the idea is to fill your day *first* with things you must get done—tasks that are more important than other "emergencies" that are likely to arise. In doing this, you take control of your time and how you spend it and are less likely to become a victim of other people's poor planning.

Without planning your day in advance, there is a higher chance it will end up looking more like this:

| | |
|---|---|
| 8:30 | Grab coffee, review incoming emails |
| 9:00 | Employee stops by for a chat |
| 9:30 | Take phone call from friend |
| 10:00 | Check email again, respond |
| 10:30 | Attend meeting you don't need to be at |
| 11:00 | Meeting still wasting your time |
| 11:30 | Make travel arrangements for next week |
| 12:00 | Lunch |
| 12:30 | Lunch |
| 1:00 | Check email |
| 1:30 | Attend another pointless meeting you don't need to attend |
| 2:00 | Still at the meeting |
| 2:30 | Check email |
| 3:00 | Check social media |

| 3:30 | Take incoming phone call from employee |
|------|----------------------------------------|
| 4:00 | Another employee stops by to chat |
| 4:30 | Skim the news |
| 5:00 | Head home |

I'm hoping this is not what your day looks like, but I suspect it may be more like it than not.

By taking charge and slotting high value, revenue-generating tasks first, you help prevent interruptions from lower priority activities. You simply don't have time in your schedule—literally—to fit them in. And that's a good thing for your productivity. You have to block out the noise.

## Maximizing Productivity

Where product-based companies generate more revenue by selling more items, service-based companies maximize revenue by increasing billable hours. The standard in the legal industry is for every 10 hours worked, eight hours can be billed; that means 80 percent of an attorney's time should be revenue-generating. I'm only saying you should shoot for 75 percent.

According to research conducted by The Alternative Board (TAB), 33 percent of entrepreneurs believe email is the biggest time suck within their job. Administrative tasks were cited as the second biggest time-waster by 24 percent of entrepreneurs.

Meetings are another unproductive use of time—think about how much a single meeting with several professionals in attendance costs your company. The number is huge. If you're an executive vice president making $150,000 a year and you're meeting with two other people who are making $65,000 each, for two hours, that meeting cost you $272, at a minimum—not taking into account any kinds of benefits. That's a lot of money for one meeting. You better have gotten a lot done.

*The Wall Street Journal* reported that the Executive Time Use Project found executives spent 18 hours of a 55-hour week in meetings. They also spent three hours on phone calls and five hours in meals, hopefully entertaining clients and prospects.

One way that I took charge of my schedule was that I didn't allow "Got a sec?" meetings. If an employee caught me in the hallway and asked, "Got a sec?" to discuss something, I would say no. Instead, I asked them to schedule a meeting with a clear purpose and agenda, making it clear what they needed from me. That way we could cut right to the chase from the beginning and I could give them what they needed in the least amount of time. Being able to get right back to work maximized my productivity and theirs, allowing us both to make more money for the company.

 *Fill your day first with things you must get done—tasks that are more important than other "emergencies" that are likely to arise.*

## Running Effective Meetings

Avoiding or significantly reducing the number of meetings you attend regularly is one way to focus your attention and your efforts, but there are some meetings where your presence is required and useful. In those meetings, you'll want to be sure you're maximizing everyone's time. To do that, try these strategies:

- **Prepare an agenda.** Identifying the topics to be covered, who is responsible for what, and what you hope to achieve is key to covering a lot of ground in as little time as possible during a meeting.
- **Identify key attendees.** Don't invite everyone to the meeting. Determine who needs to be there in order to have the best

outcome, whether that's a decision or information gathering. Then invite the essential participants only.

- **Start and end on time**. It's easy for meetings to extend beyond the designated window, so don't let them. Wrap up at the designated end time—or earlier.
- **Stay focused on the topic of discussion**. Some experts advocate creating a "parking lot," which is where unrelated topics that are mentioned are written down for later research and potential discussion. This helps keep discussions on-topic and the meeting running efficiently.
- **Follow up**. Prepare and disseminate a summary of what was discussed and who is responsible for what next steps, as well as any future meeting dates.

Since meetings are generally not part of the 75 percent of your time that should be devoted to revenue generation, do your best to reduce the amount of time spent in them and to maximize your productivity within the meetings you do have to attend.

Work each day on your revenue-producing activities and don't leave until they're done. That's how you'll move your business well ahead of the competition.

## Speed Read

- Use your money sheet to quickly see how you're progressing toward reaching your monthly revenue target. Complete your six to eight top priorities before you leave each day. Fill your schedule with those tasks first, to limit the amount of time other tasks can take up.
- Eliminate meetings that truly don't require your attendance. Too many business owners waste the majority of their day in them.

- For meetings that are essential, ask for a purpose, an agenda, and a clear definition of the desired deliverable. Don't attend meetings that don't require your input—that would be a waste of your time and a lot of money.

# Overdeliver for Your Customers

By focusing on revenue generation, your company will earn more money and you can afford to overdeliver for your customers. Providing the ultimate customer service experience will cost you more money, but long-term it's the key to dominating your market.

We now live in a world where people are much less loyal to brands. After all, there are millions of them to choose from. Think about the number of brand choices you make in a day—Starbucks or Tim Horton's for your morning coffee, Exxon or British Petroleum for gasoline, Bic or Mont Blanc for pens, Rolex or Tag Heuer for your watch, Cheesecake Factory or Chipotle for lunch, Stitch Fix or Trunk Club for clothing selection—you get the idea. You probably make multiple brand choices on an hourly basis.

The selection of products within each brand name is also massive. Instead of one or two major brands, consumers now may have 10 or 20 to choose from. Look at laundry detergent for example; the number of brands that P&G owns alone is staggering. Competition is fierce.

New companies are also popping up so fast that brands can rise and fall in short order. Take Klout, for example, the app that aspired to rate users based on influence. The more influential you were online, the higher your Klout score. Started in 2008, Klout peaked around 2012, industry observers say, was nearly irrelevant by 2014 and was shut down in 2018. That's a pretty steep rise and fall, all made possible by the Internet.

## The Rise of the Consumer Review

Brand loyalty is a thing of the past, with more decisions being made based on recommendations of others. Where newspaper and magazine articles were one of the top sources of product information a decade or two ago, ahead of paid advertisements, today product reviews are among the top drivers of purchase decisions. In fact, many customers rely on the opinions of strangers when buying a product for the first time.

Yelp pioneered restaurant reviews, encouraging folks dining out to snap photos of their meals and share their opinions regarding the whole dining experience. From dining reviews we shifted to travel reviews, from hotel accommodations to airline travel to excursions on sites like TripAdvisor. And from there reviews went mainstream.

Many purchase decisions today are made by consumers asking the following questions:

- Is it good? (What do other customers say about it?)
- Do my friends think it's good? (What are people saying about it on social media?)
- How fast can I get it? (Amazon Prime has conditioned customers to expect two-day delivery of their orders)

As a result, positive reviews have become an influential part of the buying process. Whether you're buying on Amazon, where reviews are a factor in where your product is ranked, on eBay, where customer feedback indicates how customer service-oriented the seller is, or some other website, ratings of how well a product performed or fit or matched the buyer's expectations are everywhere.

A survey by Dimensional Research a couple of years ago found that 90 percent of consumers who recalled reading an online review reported that it influenced their behavior. And 86 percent said the same thing about negative reviews—they influenced their purchase decision. Those are big numbers that underscore how important reviews have become.

And services aren't immune to customer reviews either. Thanks to social media, Google, and YouTube, customers of everything from appliance repair to accounting to transportation—such as Uber and Lyft—have the opportunity to rate and review their service provider. In some cases, those reviews have a direct impact on their earning potential.

## Customers Have More Power

Customers now have significantly more power in the sales transaction thanks to the importance of reviews. If a customer doesn't like what they've purchased, they expect the seller to make them happy, whether that means accepting a return, providing a replacement, or offering a refund (and sometimes all three, depending on the customer). The onus is on the business to satisfy the customer, or risk receiving an—often very public—negative review.

Most companies don't want that. One negative review that goes viral can be damaging to a business' reputation and discourage others from buying.

Of course, there are smart ways and stupid ways to handle this. The Union Street Guest House, a hotel in Hudson, New York, tried to clamp down on negative reviews by notifying brides and grooms that any negative reviews of the hotel left by wedding guests would result in a $500 charge to the happy couple. Needless to say, once word got out that this was the hotel's policy, there was plenty of negative publicity and the company backed down. Don't do this.

Yes, you should most definitely respond to a negative review and try and explain the circumstances, in a polite and friendly way, so that anyone who reads the negative will see your explanation (notice I didn't say "excuse"). For example, if a customer complains that your offset printing operation got the color wrong in her brochure and refused to reprint them for free, you can use the reply feature that most reviews allow to explain your position. Perhaps the customer reviewed the blueline and the comp and signed off on the color two times before you went to press, assuming the responsibility for the wrong color at that time. You offered to reprint at a discounted rate and he refused, you can explain.

Or, maybe you were at fault. Don't let the negative review go unanswered in that case either. Reply and apologize profusely, take responsibility, and offer much more than a refund to compensate the customer for the aggravation. Maybe repeat the service at no charge and refund the original purchase price, or something like that. The key is to be polite, understanding, and apologetic.

That's what other potential customers are looking for—how you handle a situation when something goes wrong. If you respond angrily, deny any culpability, and treat the customer poorly, you're digging your own grave. No one is going to want to do business with you.

A prime example of this is what went down at the Radiator Doctor in California. Customer Brandon gave the auto repair shop a bad review and the owner responded with a rant that included snide remarks and insults. Not the way to convince customers that Brandon's experience was a fluke.

But if you use the opportunity to correct the mistake and are able to delight the customer, you may even be able to convince them to remove the negative review altogether. However, don't ask for that until you're sure they're extremely pleased with how you rectify the problem.

 *Ninety percent of consumers who recalled reading an online review reported that it influenced their behavior.*

### How to Overdeliver

Of course, the best solution is to avoid this reactive situation altogether—do all you can to inspire your customers to write glowing, sincere positive reviews. Overdeliver in every facet of your business. Here are some ideas for how to do this:

- **Make sure the customer buying experience is easy**. Don't require six steps if you can complete the transaction in four. Offer several payment options to make the purchase as convenient as possible for the customer. Sure, you may not have a Diners Club card, but if your customer wants to use it, you should allow it.
- **Make it simple and obvious how to ask questions**. Use Live Chat to allow customers to get details while they're in buying mode. And offer other ways to get in touch, too, like phone and email.
- **Make returns easy**. Who cares why someone wants to return something?! Accept the return, make sure the return process is easy, and refund quickly. Don't make the customer fill out form after form to return their purchase.
- **Keep customers informed**. Use email to communicate regarding the status of their order without going overboard. Daily emails aren't necessary—only when their order has

moved closer to being delivered. And don't add customers to your email list without their express permission. They may have bought something from you as a gift and have no interest in follow-up emails.

- **Offer a product/service guarantee**. Thanks to companies like LL Bean and The North Face, which accept product returns without a huge hassle, customers now expect a no-questions-asked return policy on everything. That's the new standard that they expect you to live up to.

- **Let customers sample your work or try your products**. Offer a small, entry-level offering to give them a sense of the quality of your workmanship, or create product samples that you provide customers with every purchase. Or offer a try-before-you-buy opportunity. For example, some online mattress companies allow customers to sleep on their mattress for 60 days before deciding whether to keep it. If they elect to return it, the process is quick and simple.

Whenever we landed a new client we would always overpromise and overdeliver. The saying underpromise and overdeliver is weak and won't allow you to land the amount and kind of clients that you want. You've got to do both.

Customers want the world and you need to give it to them. If I sold a digital marketing program that consisted of one landing page and ongoing paid media and SEO, I would make sure that we delivered two versions of the landing page, banner ads, and a test plan. I always gave them more than they paid for.

Did it cost me a little more? Sure. But I worked so hard to land that account that I was going to continue to work hard to ensure I kept it. Customers are not loyal any more to brands, they are only loyal to results. You need to overpromise and overdeliver if you want to scale with speed and grow a monster business.

The challenge is that you have to overdeliver in every aspect of your business, not just in one or two. That is, you can't provide amazing customer service but a crappy product. Or maybe your service quality is the best on the market, but you're scheduling six months out—no one's going to want to wait that long.

You need to deliver the best available:

- Service
- Speed
- Quality

In the past, the joke was that customers had to choose two of the following three elements: speed, quality, or cost. You couldn't have all three, but you could have two.

Today, customers want and expect all three. And the better you're able to give it to them, the better your online reviews and your customer satisfaction levels. That's how you'll overdeliver for your customers.

## Speed Read
- Customers today are nearly overwhelmed with the variety and breadth of product and service brands available. They are much less brand loyal and much more willing to make a switch. So getting new customers is easier and holding onto existing ones more difficult.
- Thanks to the prominence and importance of online reviews, customers have a lot more power. They can directly impact your business reputation depending on the review they give your company.

- Delighting your customers by working to deliver more than they ever expected from you will significantly increase your odds of getting more positive reviews. Overdelivering on your promises reduces the odds of receiving negative reviews and potentially builds up a stockpile of positive ones that will negate any possible negative ones that come up.

# Only Measure What Matters

**M**easurement is essential as you learn how to tweak, evolve, and change rapidly. A measurement framework is critical in order to scale with speed because without measurement you're not able to pivot, optimize, and adjust the good and the bad.

How well is your company doing? How do you know? You may personally feel great about your progress and results, but you can't really tell how your business is performing against the goals you've set unless you're measuring key performance indicators (also known as KPIs). By tracking and routinely checking the following business metrics, you can quickly see where you're excelling and spot what may need attention.

1. **Digital Micro-Conversions**

How well your company is attracting prospects is your first performance indicator. These are micro-conversions, or actions prospects take that indicate interest in what your company does or what you sell.

Micro-conversions include:

- Website traffic—How many people are looking for, finding, and visiting your website?
- Newsletter subscribers—How many people learn about your company, read your content, and want to be sure not to miss future newsletters by subscribing?
- Freebie downloads—How many people hand over their name and email address so that you can send them information that is of interest to them?
- YouTube views—How many people take the time to watch your YouTube videos related to your business? Is that number rising or falling?
- Social media followers—How many people have liked your Facebook page or posts, how many Instagram followers do you have, or LinkedIn connections? Are you attracting eyeballs?

The steps that potential customers have taken to connect with your business are micro-conversions and could lead to a future purchase. Numbers that are increasing month-over-month suggest rising interest in what you're selling while falling micro-conversions may indicate there's a problem somewhere in your sales process.

If that's the case, the good news is that you've been alerted to the issue early enough to be able to address it before it impacts your sales figures.

*Out of 26 unhappy customers, only one will bother to tell you directly that they're unhappy.*

## Qualified Leads in Pipeline

It can be difficult to think about marketing when all your time and attention is focused on serving the customers you have right now, but in order for your company to survive and thrive, you need to have a constant pipeline of new business leads flowing through.

From your micro-conversions come your leads, or people who have a stated interested in your product or service. They move into your sales pipeline, which is your process for turning leads into qualified leads and then into customers. However, not every lead is likely to become a customer—some leads are "tire-kickers," or people who are curious but not truly serious about making a purchase. They may come into your sales funnel and get weeded out. That's okay, it's how a funnel works.

If they're not qualified it's because they don't match your ideal customer profile. That could be because they live outside your service area, so you can't help them even if you wanted to, because they can't afford your price, or maybe because they don't meet your minimum requirements for company size, if you're a business-to-business (B2B) marketer.

One way to easily monitor what qualified leads you have in your pipeline at the moment, and the potential impact they could have on your bottom line is to use a simple spreadsheet that tracks who they are, what they're worth, and when they're likely to become customers. It could look something like this:

| Lead Name | $ Value of Business | % Chance You'll Win Business | Projected Impact on Business | When Expected to Close |
|---|---|---|---|---|
| Cathy, IBM | $250,000 | 50% | $125,000 | 5/2019 |
| | | | | |
| | | | | |
| | | | | |
| | | | | |
| | | | | |
| | | | | |

You'll want to keep track of how many total leads and qualified leads you receive each month. Ideally, over time you'll see an increasing percentage of qualified leads—potential customers you want to do business with—and fewer unqualified leads that use up resources you could have invested in converting qualified leads to customers.

## 2. Conversion Rate

The percentage of qualified leads that turn into customers determines your conversion rate. For example, if you had 100 qualified leads last month and 20 became customers, your conversion rate is 20 percent. (Divide the number of new customers by the number of qualified leads for that same period to get your conversion rate.)

To optimize your conversion rate you need to consider what has an impact on a lead's willingness to buy. Is it your offer? Your pricing? Your product features? Your turnaround time? Your marketing message? Something else?

The only way to know is to test it—changing one factor at a time and tracking which offer, price, feature mix, etc., drives the highest conversion rate.

205 | Only Measure What Matters

3. **Customer Acquisition Cost (CAC)**

To make sure you don't go broke chasing new customers, you need to carefully watch your customer acquisition cost (CAC), or what it costs you to win a new customer. It's typically impossible to link marketing expenses back to each individual customer, but you can certainly take the total amount you spent on marketing and divide that figure by how many new customers you landed for a particular time period.

If you spent, let's say, $10,000 last month on marketing and you acquired 100 new customers, your CAC is $100. That's great if the average customer purchase costs more than $100, but if your average purchase is $30, you're losing money with every new customer.

Keep in mind, however, that you don't want to consider only the first purchase a customer makes, but, rather, how much they'll spend during their lifetime with you (customer lifetime value, or CLV).

This is important, especially if you sell a product or service that is recurring, such as maid service, food and drinks at a restaurant, a monthly software subscription, or cars. If you do a good job the first time, it's very likely your customer will come back and buy from you again.

So based on the average frequency of purchase—which is probably weekly if you're selling groceries and every five years if you're selling houses—you can calculate the lifetime value of your customers.

Let's look at the value of a real estate customer as an example. Since we're likely to move every 11.4 years and the average American home costs $207,600, a Realtor™ earning 3 percent on every purchase or sale could pocket $6,228 per sale. Over the lifetime of a customer, those 11.4 moves could generate $70,999. Obviously, selling higher value homes or homes more frequently can significantly increase a customer's value.

Keep that in mind as you assess how much you're paying to land a new customer, and how that number changes over time. You always want to be sure you're paying less to acquire a customer than that customer's lifetime value.

4. **Customer Retention**

While many businesses focus on obtaining new customers as their main strategy for growth, an even more important number to watch is your customer retention rate. It's much easier to keep an existing customer than it is to win a new one—and far less costly. Experts estimate that it costs six to seven times more to win a new customer than to hold onto one you already have.

If you're constantly losing customers, you may find it very difficult to be profitable.

To monitor your customer retention rate, you need three numbers:

- Number of customers you had at the beginning of a time period (usually one year)
- Number of new customers acquired during that same period
- Number of customers at the end of that same period

To help with the math, let's say that you had 50 customers on January 1, got 80 new ones throughout the year, and had 60 on December 31. That means you retained 60-80/50 * 100 = -40 percent. That's horrible.

Given that negative rate, you'll want to look at what you're doing to serve your customers and take steps to improve your product or service before you spend more money trying to attract more customers.

On the other hand, if you started with 25 customers, added another 25 during the year, and ended up with 48 customers, your retention rate would be a terrific 92 percent (48-25/25 * 100 = 92 percent).

Watch your customer retention rate closely to be sure your customers are continuing to be satisfied with the quality of products, services, and level of customer service you deliver.

5. **Net Promoter Score**

You've probably heard that customers who are unhappy with their purchase experience may not tell you, but they'll sure tell all their friends! In fact, 96 percent of your unhappy customers won't say anything, but they'll tell 15 friends. A study by TARP reported that out of 26 unhappy customers, only one will bother to tell you directly that they're unhappy.

This is important, because to be successful, you need customers who love what you do and are so thrilled that they rave about your business to all their friends. That's not going to happen if they aren't wowed. Keeping customers happy is critical for your long-term success.

Your Net Promoter Score is a measure of what percent of your customers are raving about you and what percent are complaining. Net Promoter Network explains that there are three levels of customer advocacy:

**Promoters** (who give you a score of nine or 10 on a 10-point scale). These are loyal customers who say positive things to their network and help increase your sales.

**Passives** (give you a score of seven or eight). These customers aren't unhappy, but they aren't thrilled either. They're likely to buy elsewhere if a better deal comes along. They're not really talking about you at all.

**Detractors** (give you a score of 0 to six). These are your dissatisfied customers who talk smack about you every chance they get. When they do this, they can damage your company's reputation.

To calculate your Net Promoter Score, subtract the number or percentage of customers who are Detractors from those who are Promoters—the passives don't really impact your Net Promoter Score so they're not part of the equation.

Regularly monitoring your Net Promoter Score is another way to be alerted when something is wrong with your product or process. Simply ask for feedback by way of a follow-up email or phone call to find out which camp each customer is in.

6. **Revenue**

Of course, your revenue is probably the fastest and easiest way to see how your company is performing. Your revenue is the total of all your sales minus any returns or refund requests.

While there are always business cycles that will impact your annual revenue, you want to see monthly revenue totals exceeding what you earned during the same period last year. That's another measure of your progress—revenue growth.

You'll also want to look at where your revenue is coming from. That is, do you have ongoing contracts that provide reoccurring revenue, or do you generate most of your revenue from projects? To scale your business, you're going to want to move more toward reoccurring revenue opportunities, which provide a solid financial foundation, rather than intermittent project income.

7. **Profit & Cash Flow**

Your profit is what's left over after you subtract all of your business expenses from your revenue for the same period. Your profit is a measure of your company's financial health.

Two ways to improve profitability are: 1) increase your revenue relative to your expenses and 2) reduce your costs. By doing one or both of these, you can increase the amount of money left over after you account for all of your business expenses.

Cash flow is the amount of money coming in to your business and the amount of money going out. If you are not effectively monitoring and measuring your cash flow you could miss loan payments, payroll or other big financial obligations. Make sure you know what you owe, when you owe it and how much cash you have on hand to pay it.

8. **90-Day Goals/Milestone Progress**

If you're reading this book, I'll assume that one of your goals is to grow your business quickly. That's your overarching goal. But in order to achieve that big picture goal, you need to break it down into shorter-term goals—kind of like the chunking we talked about earlier.

On top of setting annual goals, also set quarterly, or 90-day goals. It's much easier to monitor and track the progress you're making toward a target goal that is three months away at the outset. That timeframe is close enough that there's pressure on to make headway daily and weekly, else you'll get too far behind.

Ninety days is long enough to accomplish some big action item, such as implementing a new CRM system or launching a new website. And then you can set new ones for another 90-day period once those goals have been met.

In your 90-day goals, you could set a target for number of new clients earned, number of website visits, employee retention rates, and even expense reductions.

Having a due date that's only three months out puts a level of pressure on to perform that a one-year or three-year goal just doesn't. That's why it's a useful timeframe for entrepreneurs—you're more likely to constantly check your progress toward that goal.

9. **Culture**

While much of our attention as entrepreneurs is focused externally, on prospects and customers who will pay us money, it's important to also monitor employee satisfaction and corporate culture.

Employees who are engaged, challenged, and feel appreciated will stick around much longer than those who are not. And since replacing an employee can cost anywhere from 16 percent of their annual salary, for high-turnover jobs, to as much as 213 percent for a highly-skilled, managerial position, according to research done by the Center for American Progress (CAP), retaining employees can have a very positive impact on your bottom line.

Regularly checking in with employees, getting to know them as people outside of work, helps make them feel connected to the organization. Not only does that increase their productivity, but that bond reduces the odds of their leaving.

So take the time to regularly chat with every employee, see what they're working on or are worried about, and let them know that they're doing a great job. Doing that will help attract and retain good employees.

Using tools to regularly track performance in various aspects of your business will let you know when things start to go off-track. From the number of leads received to new customers earned to profitability and employee retention, you can learn a lot about the direction your business is headed by routinely monitoring key performance indicators.

### Speed Read

- Use free metrics, such as Google Analytics and Google Alerts to regularly track all the aspects of your business that drive growth.
- Compare numbers year-over-year and month-over-month to account for seasonality or cyclicality in your revenue.
- Have a mix of both quantitative—revenue, profits, net promoter score—and qualitative—satisfaction levels, 90-day goals—to measure progress toward your goals.

# Always Be Testing and Optimizing

Test and optimize constantly. No matter how well you're doing, if you're not testing every outcome you'll never be able to improve on it. If you want to scale with speed you have to test to grow and improve.

Most organizations are more like the Titanic than the nimble Cigarette boat. It takes far longer to adjust the course of a massive ship than it does to turn a leaner, sleeker speed machine. You want to be a performance racer, not an ocean liner.

To be more successful, you need to move quickly, producing a steady stream of new ideas. The more new products, services, updates, or enhancements you introduce, the more distance you'll put between your business and your competition.

*You can make progress faster by tweaking elements along the way, rather than attempting to make it perfect.*

### Don't Get Left Behind

In 1998, Nokia was the world's largest mobile phone brand. It was the 800-lb. gorilla of cell phones and was way ahead of its competition in terms of R&D and new product development. In fact, says Gizmodo, "In the late 1990s, Nokia predicted the future of mobile: it spent millions on research, and even demonstrated touch-screen devices that closely resembled today's iPhones and Androids."

It also had developed a table computer with a wireless connection and touch screen that looks a lot like Apple's iPad, reported the *Wall Street Journal*.

Apparently management didn't realize what it had and continued to research and develop without a real plan to introduce its products to consumers. Says the *Wall Street Journal*:

> "Nokia actually developed the sorts of devices that consumers are gobbling up today. It just didn't bring them to market. In a strategic blunder, it shifted its focus from smartphones back to basic phones right as the iPhone upended the market."

"Nokia should have moved off its smartphone platform Symbian and onto its next-generation platform, MeeGo, much sooner than it did," says TechCrunch. But it didn't, and it took quite a while for the company to begin to realize its misstep.

When Apple debuted the iPhone, did Nokia scramble, realizing the lead it had lost? No, it did not. Instead, its CEO, Olli-Pekka Kallasvuo, stated that they "welcomed" Apple entering the market and suspected it would stimulate demand for phones in general:

*"I don't think that what we have seen so far (from Apple) is something that would any way necessitate us changing our thinking when it comes to openness, our software and business approach."*

Yup, he was dead wrong.

Nokia blew its lead of seven years, gave it up to Apple, and watched its market share plummet from 40 percent to just 3 percent of the global smartphone market by 2013.

It rested on its laurels and eventually had to sell what was left of its assets to Microsoft while they were still worth something.

## Become an Idea-Generating Machine

So how, exactly, do you build this agile, creative organization capable of generating a steady stream of new ideas? It's all about the process you have in place to come up with new concepts, test them, and roll them out.

To set up your organization to have always testing environment, use this framework:

1. **Brainstorm ideas.** Challenge yourself or those on your team to come up with new and innovative products or solutions—whatever your company needs at the moment.

Schedule a brainstorming session and ask everyone to come to the meeting with three ideas to propose, suggests Ken Hudson in *The Idea Generator*. That way, you start the discussion with creative ideas, rather than trying to force everyone to be brilliant on the spot and unprepared.

Try to come up with as many approaches or concepts first—without editing or analysis—and then go back and evaluate later, so as to keep the ideas flowing.

2. **Gather competitive intelligence**. New ideas in hand, now see what the competition is up to. What are they working on or about to announce? Where is their attention focused?

Some great places to find this information include:

- Trade shows and conferences. Listen to the chatter, pick up materials, ask questions of speakers and attendees. Study corporate websites and marketing campaigns—where they are spending and what their ads look like. Use Similarweb to better understand your competitors' marketing messaging and where they are spending online.
- Job boards. What kinds of openings does the competition have? Does this suggest a new initiative, perhaps?
- Analyst reports. If your business operates in an industry that financial analysts cover, you may be able to obtain published analyses of market share breakdowns, gains and losses, and coming developments.
- Google and PRNewswire. The real objective of this step isn't to know everything there is to know about all your competitors, but to get a general sense of where their attention is focused and whether it will impact your company's ability to make a market move. You do not want to compete. You want to dominate. So you have to bring better ideas, products, and services to the marketplace so you crush your competition.

3. **Estimate product creation costs**. You have some killer ideas, but what will they cost to implement? That is, how much time will they take to develop, how much money will it take to be successful, and what value will those ideas generate? Does the

cost and commitment of resources justify the effort, given the value to be created? What I often like to ask is, is the juice worth the squeeze?

4. **Determine your goal**. Before rushing to design and launch a new product or service, take a step back and confirm your ultimate goal. Are you trying to gauge market interest for a potential new product or are you ready to proceed with actual production? Is your objective information-gathering and research or a new market entrant?

5. **Validate the concept**. The only way to know if you're on to something and have the makings of a winning offering is to ask your target market. The best way to do that is to conduct quick and cost-effective market research. You can ask for feedback from prospects and customers online to get their reaction to everything from product features, service costs, perceived value, and even marketing campaigns, to make sure what you're planning to introduce is of interest and/or likely to be purchased by your audience.

6. **Release the first generation**. Rolling out your new product or service is the best way to get market feedback. What features are dubbed "a Godsend" and which are panned? What do customers love about it and what is generating complaints? What suggestions do they have for improvement?

7. **Iterate and improve**. Use the feedback from people who tried or purchased your product or service to make it better in subsequent versions.

Some publishers plan small initial print runs of new books, recognizing that typos and errors within the manuscript will be discovered by readers once released, followed by larger subsequent print runs once the errors are caught and corrected.

The first generation of TiVo digital video recorders introduced in 1998 were immediately loved by customers. The ability to record TV shows and movies and skip through commercials was a welcome development, but the fact that you could only record one channel at a time was a limitation customers griped about. So in later models, TiVo has continually expanded the number of channels that can be recorded simultaneously.

Experts talk about building the plane while flying it—getting it aloft and then making improvements en route, rather than waiting until the plane has been pilot-tested and approved. That's a smart approach for success-driven entrepreneurs.

You can make progress faster by tweaking elements along the way, rather than attempting to make it perfect. Accept the fact that it probably won't ever be perfect—that's an unrealistic goal—and strive for the next best level of performance.

## How to Encourage More Ideas

Companies that are known for innovation and revolutionary thinking, such as Apple, Amazon, and Tesla, have created an internal culture that rewards idea generation. To encourage more idea generation in your own business, try these ideas to spark new concepts:

- Pair seemingly disparate ideas together. Think fried ice cream, for example, or tape that doesn't permanently stick to surfaces.
- Envision the ideal solution and its components. What would the perfect answer look like?
- Define the opposite of what you want. Want a non-toxic cleanser? What are the worst ingredients that you could use and what are their functions? Now, how could you replace them?
- Try brainwriting, an approach proposed by Kellogg professors Leigh Thompson and Loran Nordgren, where team members

write their ideas down, rather than sharing them with the group, to try and ensure all ideas are heard.

- Test out reverse brainstorming, where instead of looking for solutions, you consider how the problem could be caused. For example, how does ice cream raise cholesterol levels?

Make idea generation part of your company's routine and create ways to recognize and reward people who put forth the most, in terms of quantity and quality.

## How to Validate Your Idea

To know whether you're on to something the market actually wants, versus something you want to create, you must ask for input.

Some of the best online tools for instant market feedback are:

- **Surveymonkey**. Perhaps the granddaddy of current online tools, Surveymonkey makes questionnaire development and sharing easy. Create short surveys for up to 100 people for free, or pay to get more responses, and SurveyMonkey performs simple statistical analyses.
- **Focusgroupit**. This free focus group tool allows you to invite people in your social network to participate and then run the group online.
- **E-Focus Groups**. While not a free tool, you can conduct online focus groups and monitor reactions via webcams and get instant reactions and results.
- **Facebook groups**. More companies are using the free Facebook Live function to gather participant feedback.
- **Google Hangouts**. Likewise, Google Hangouts is another free video tool for interacting with and gathering online feedback in real time.

The key to validating your idea, or not, is proposing a new product, service, or solution, and asking for feedback from potential customers. Listen to their input, take their suggestions, and encourage constructive criticism. You need to hear the good, the bad, and the ugly about your latest creation before you invest thousands or hundreds of thousands of dollars introducing it to the market.

### Pivot

The good news is, if the results of your research suggest you're not on the right path for success, you can pivot—change course, take another tack. And the earlier you get word regarding the need to do that, the faster you can make adjustments.

Negative feedback from your market research doesn't mean you need to give up, only that your current product or service iteration isn't optimal. So make it better.

### Don't Fear Failure

The only entrepreneurs who never fail are those who will never win big. The most successful are those who are willing to fail in order to learn how to succeed.

James Dyson failed 5,126 times over 15 years before developing a bagless vacuum cleaner prototype that worked.

Harland Sanders, better known as Colonel Sanders of KFC fame, failed 1,009 times to interest a restaurant in selling his fried chicken. Once he did, at age 65, Sanders made a deal to be paid 5 cents for every piece of his chicken sold. Nine years later, he had 600 franchises selling his trademarked chicken recipe.

Milton Hershey started three different candy companies, all of which failed, before establishing the Lancaster Caramel Company and the Hershey Company, which didn't.

Nine out of 10 startups fail—that means 90 percent of the time, you won't succeed. But do you stop trying? No, you charge forward and make it happen. I often tell entrepreneurs that they will fail often and need to recover faster.

Lonnie Johnson was actually tinkering with a design for an environmentally-friendly heat pump when he inadvertently invented the Super Soaker water gun. But even after developing a prototype, it took seven more years for it to be successful. By 1991, sales of the water gun exceeded $200 million and it was named one of the top 20 bestselling toys.

To succeed in the long run, you need a willingness to fail and a corporate culture that encourages risk-taking. Celebrating failure leads to learning and innovation much more frequently than never coloring outside the lines.

## Speed Read

- Instead of researching every idea to the nth degree, be brave enough to test a concept early on. Don't attempt to make your new product or service polished and perfect—it won't be.
- Develop an internal process that encourages and rewards constant brainstorming and idea generation.
- Pressure test the ideas that appear to have the greatest promise.
- Modify and tweak your initial design based on customer feedback.

# It's a Sprint, Not a Marathon

We're in a society where instant is the new standard. We've given you the secret formula to maintain this pace and scale with speed.

Once you reach peak speed in terms of business growth, it can be challenging to stay there—to continue working at that pace. The key is that once you start to achieve success, you can't deviate from the process that got you there. You need to continue doing what you've been doing, using the tools that helped you scale.

That means you need to start with your end game—what is your long-term objective? Are you building a business to sell for maximum profit in five or 10 years? Are you growing a business that you can then hand down to your kids, and their kids? Or are you creating an enterprise to pay your bills? You need to be clear about what you're doing and why in order to reap massive rewards. That clarity enables focus.

Then you need to pick your niche, choosing to be a specialist rather than a generalist. Going deep in a narrow market niche allows you to own it, to control it. That's what enables fast revenue growth. When you're competing with dozens or even hundreds of other companies operating in your market, it's hard to distinguish yourself and your offerings. But when you're the big fish in a small pond, business almost comes to you. You attract it because of your reputation and expertise.

> *It's a full-on sprint if you want to scale with speed. You must work at a different pace than everyone else if you want to succeed.*

Once you're clear about the type of business you're trying to build and the market niche you intend to serve, it's time for action—executing with speed. This is where many businesses fall short—they plan, they strategize, they meet, they discuss, they review, but they don't place a high priority on execution. To scale with speed, fast action is the most important part of the equation. Decide fast and act fast!

As your business starts to gain steam, having the right people on your team will become even more important. Find the best people, hire them, and treat them right and they will never want to leave. Those are the core steps to energizing a culture. And when employees feel valued and appreciated and challenged, those positive feelings foster a positive and productive environment.

Finally, with everything you need in place to scale with speed, it's time for focused action—for becoming obsessed with revenue generation, overdelivering for your customers, and carefully measuring your performance to be able to tweak it for even better results.

You can't get complacent. There's someone coming up behind you who's willing to work harder and longer, so you'll need to work faster to stay ahead of the pack.

### It's a Race

You've no doubt heard that adage that, "It's a marathon, not a sprint." Yeah, that's a lie. It's a full-on sprint if you want to scale with speed. You must work at a different pace than everyone else if you want to succeed.

That means, looking ahead, you need to continue to identify other opportunities for recurring revenue and expanding your current offerings through complementary products and services. But don't expand aggressively until you're the established market leader. Stay within your niche to maintain and increase profitability. Don't stretch into new businesses—that's not how you got here and not how you'll progress. You need to stay hyper-focused on serving your niche market better than anyone else.

Refer back to your one-page attack plan regularly, to stay on the correct course.

And value your time. It's the only thing you can't ever get more of. If you want to be successful, the choices you make with respect to your time are critical. Don't waste what you're given. You can waste money, because that you can make more of, but whatever you do, don't waste your time. That's a finite resource.

I know you can do this.

Make it happen!

### Speed Read

- Now that you've begun to scale with speed, don't deviate from the plan. Don't mess with what's working.
- It's not the time to expand. Instead, double down on your current, hyper-focused strategy to make real strides and keep the competition in your rear view mirror.
- It's a sprint, not a marathon. Taking a long-term view is good, but you also need to focus on the short-term to-do's to see real results.

# Morgan James
# Speakers Group

We connect Morgan James published authors with live and online events and audiences who will benefit from their expertise.